CLASSIC POP/ROCK HITS

> — PIANO LEVEL —
> EARLY INTERMEDIATE/INTERMEDIATE
> (HLSPL LEVEL 4-5)

ISBN 978-1-4234-3697-3

HAL•LEONARD® CORPORATION

7777 W. BLUEMOUND RD. P.O. BOX 13819 MILWAUKEE, WI 53213

Visit Hal Leonard Online at
www.halleonard.com

Visit Phillip at
www.phillipkeveren.com

PREFACE

The piano has played a central role in the development of pop music for many decades. The original recordings of each song in this collection featured the piano (and/or myriad keyboards) prominently. From the simple elegance of Carol King's "So Far Away" to the over-the-top drama of Queen's "Bohemian Rhapsody," the piano has provided the key element in hit after hit.

I hope you enjoy playing these classic pop songs… at the piano, of course.

Sincerely,
Phillip Keveren

◆

BIOGRAPHY

Phillip Keveren, a multi-talented keyboard artist and composer, has composed original works in a variety of genres from piano solo to symphonic orchestra. Mr. Keveren gives frequent concerts and workshops for teachers and their students in the United States, Canada, Europe, and Asia. Mr. Keveren holds a B.M. in composition from California State University Northridge and a M.M. in composition from the University of Southern California.

CONTENTS

4

BOHEMIAN RHAPSODY

Words and Music by
FREDDIE MERCURY
Arranged by Phillip Keveren

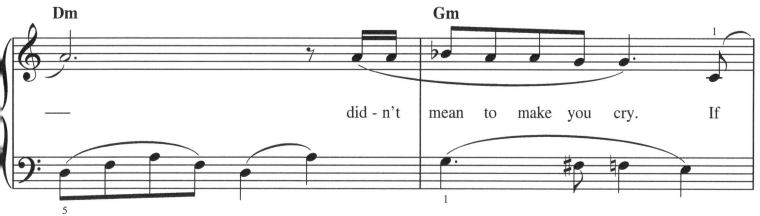

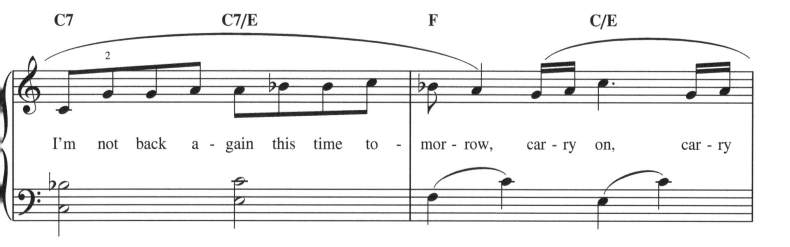

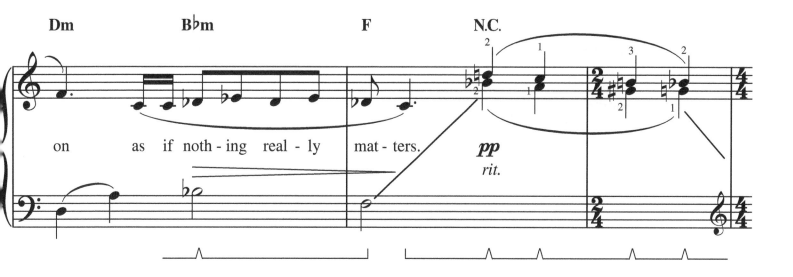

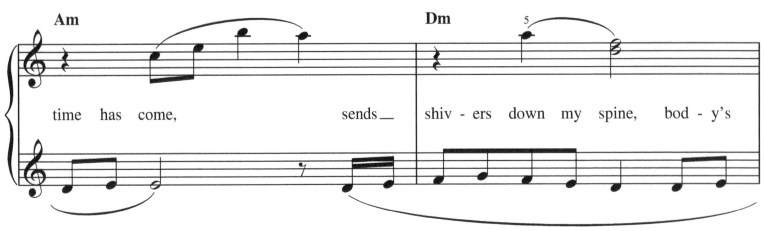

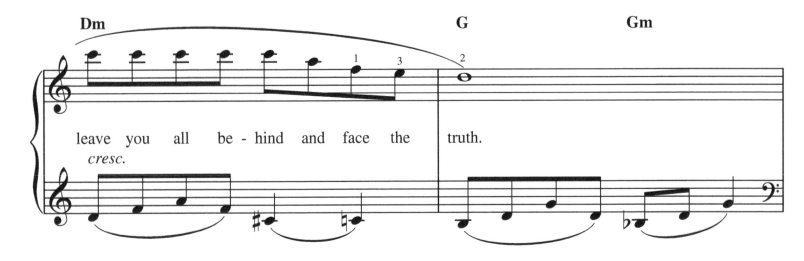

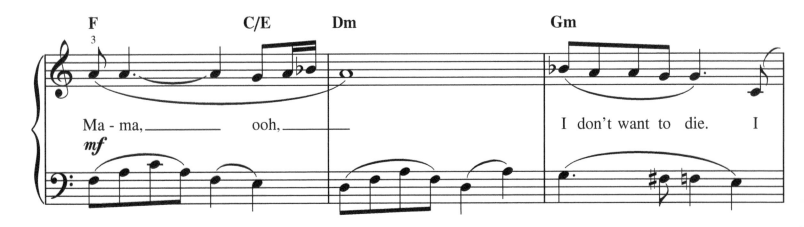

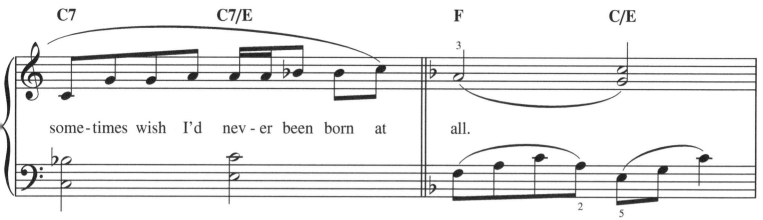

some-times wish I'd nev-er been born at all.

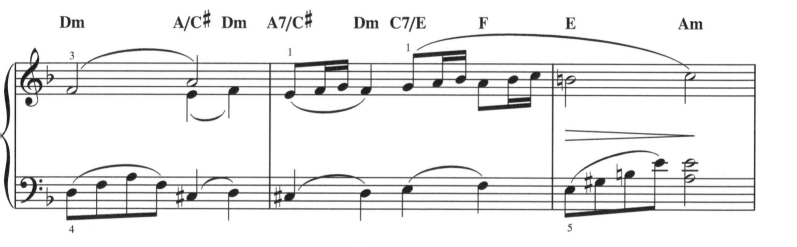

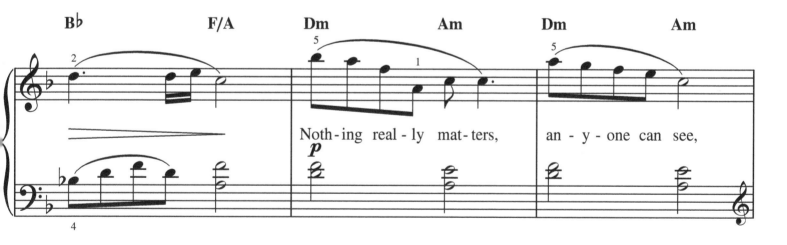

Noth-ing real-ly mat-ters, an-y-one can see,

p

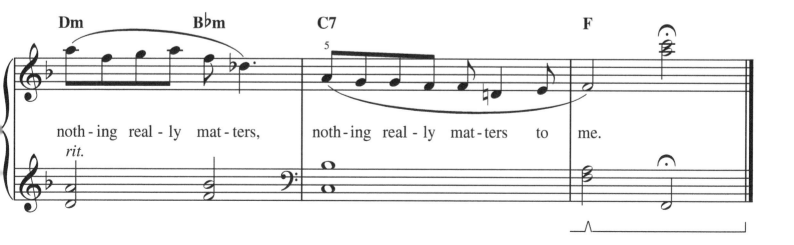

noth-ing real-ly mat-ters, nothing real-ly mat-ters to me.

rit.

DON'T KNOW MUCH

Words and Music by BARRY MANN,
CYNTHIA WEIL and TOM SNOW
Arranged by Phillip Keveren

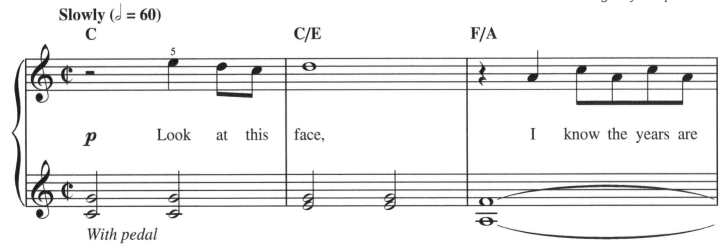

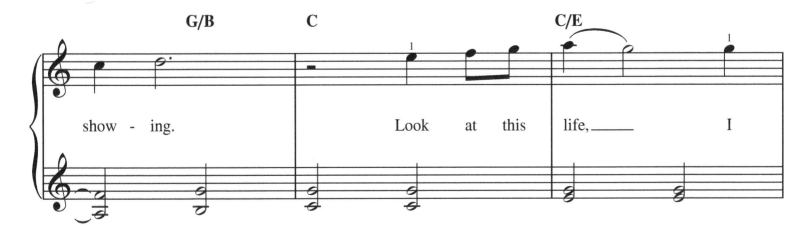

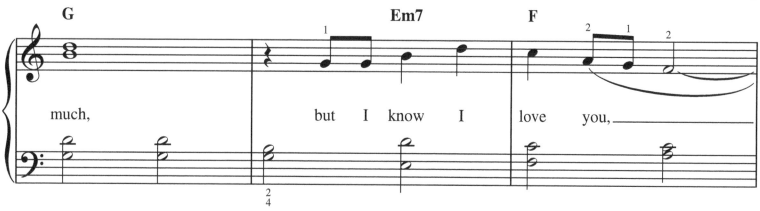

much, but I know I love you,

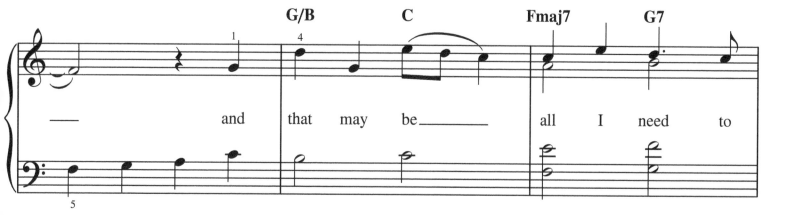

— and that may be all I need to

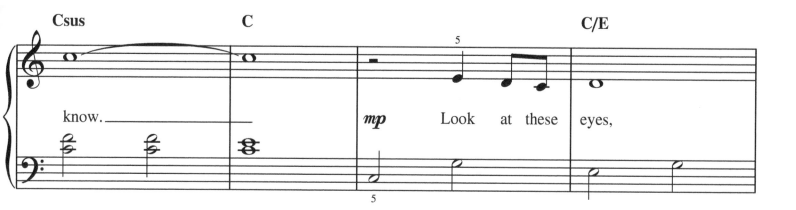

know. Look at these eyes,

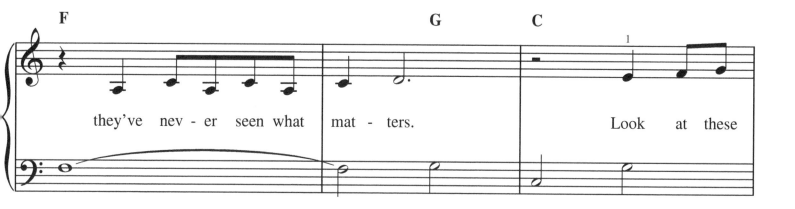

they've nev - er seen what mat - ters. Look at these

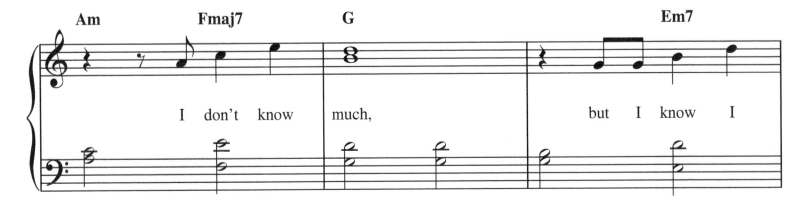

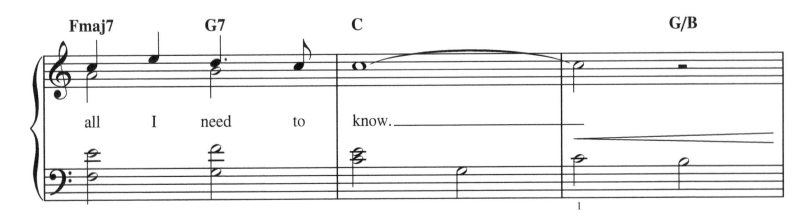

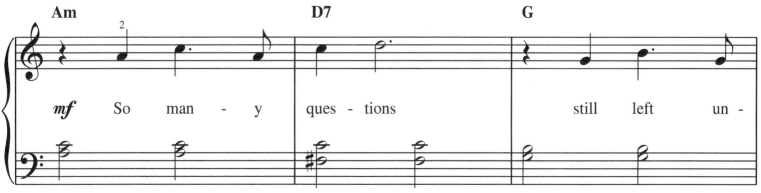

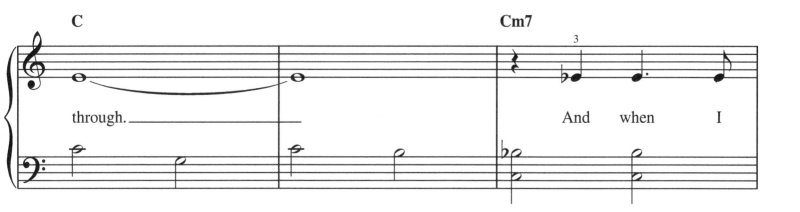

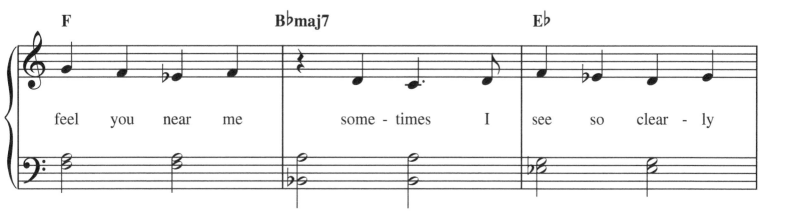

the on - ly truth I've ev - er known is me and

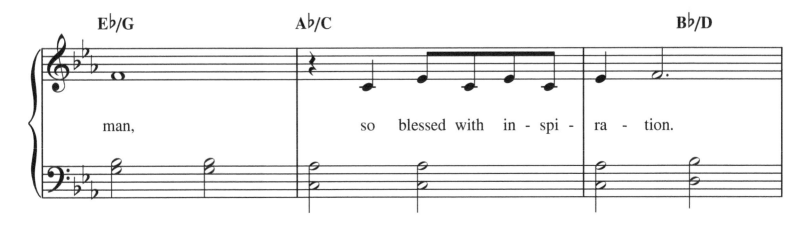

you. Look at this

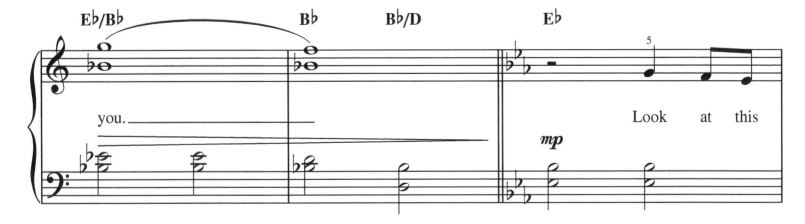

man, so blessed with in - spi - ra - tion.

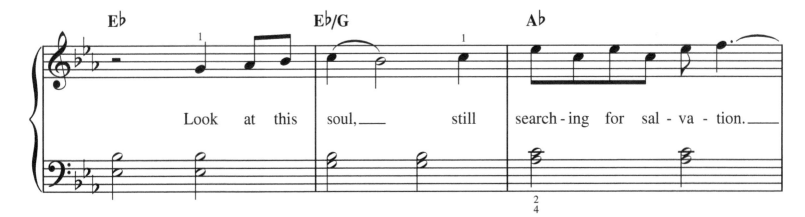

Look at this soul, still search - ing for sal - va - tion.

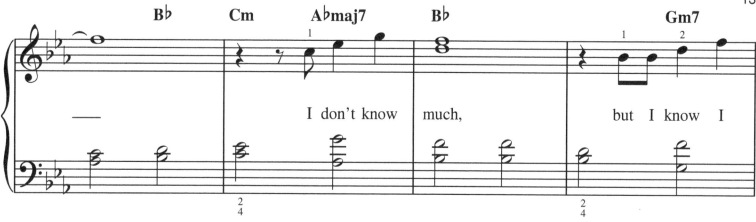

I don't know much, but I know I

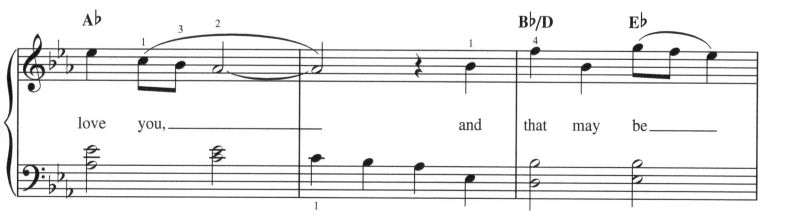

love you,_____ and that may be_____

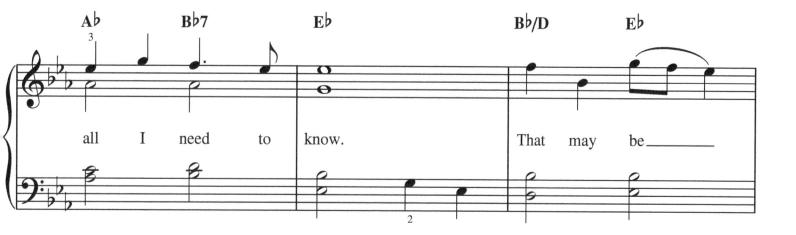

all I need to know. That may be_____

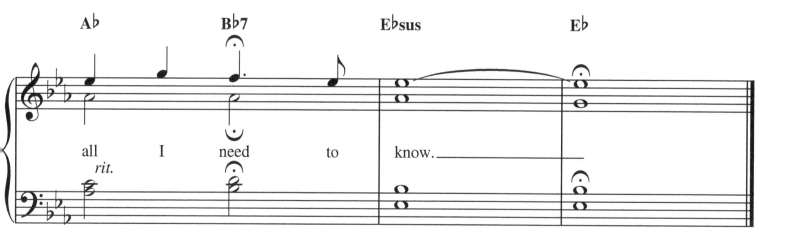

all I need to know._____

FROM A DISTANCE

Words and Music by
JULIE GOLD
Arranged by Phillip Keveren

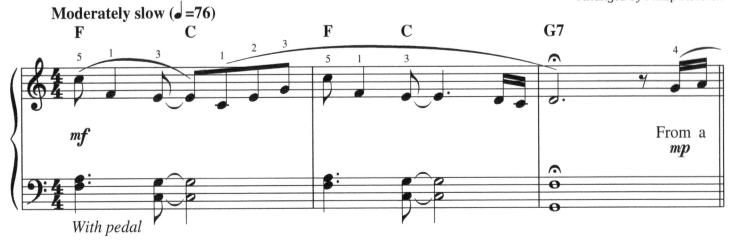

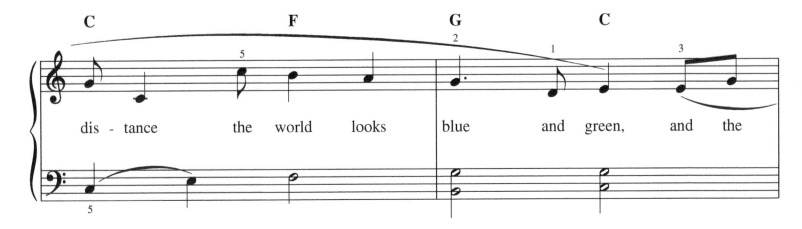

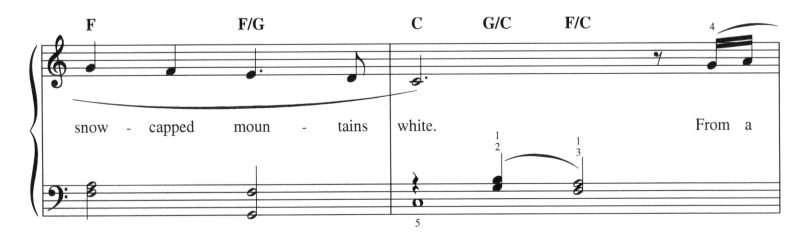

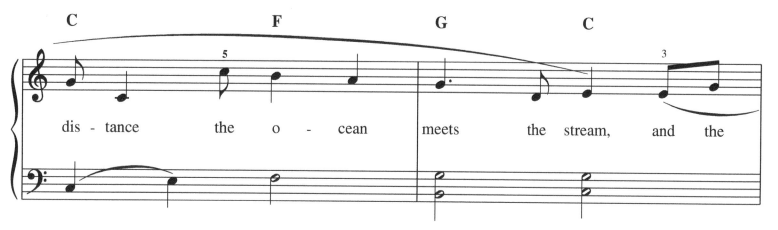

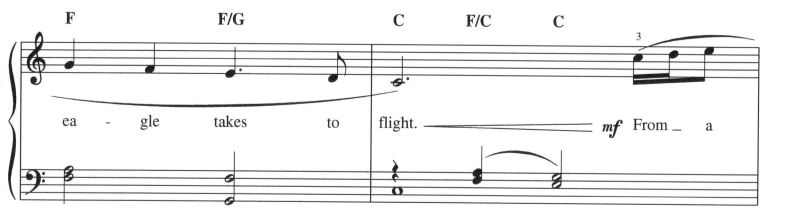

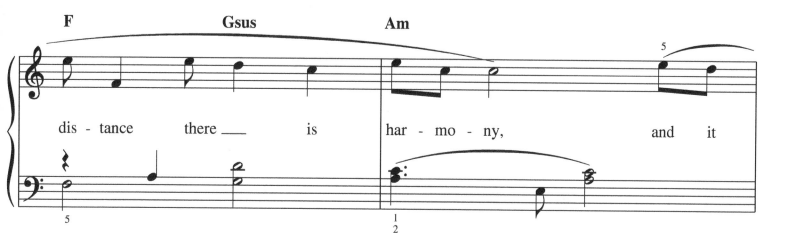

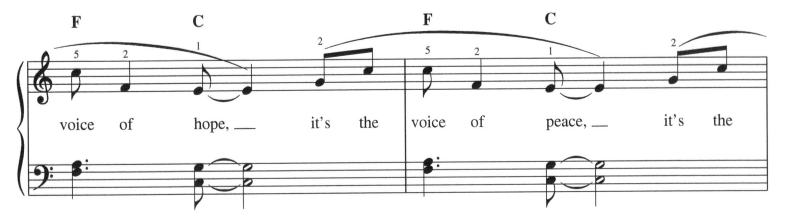

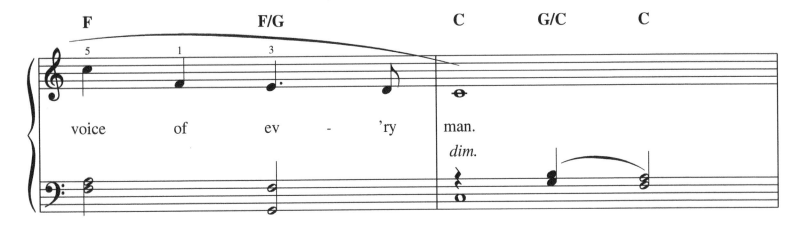

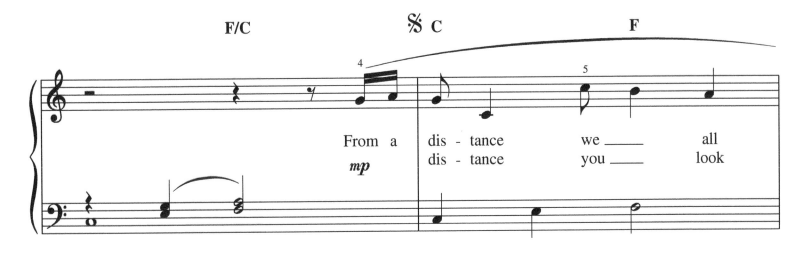

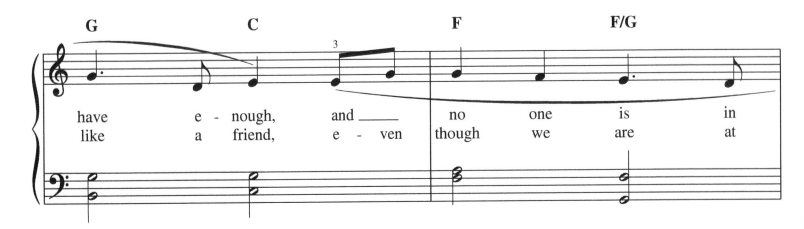

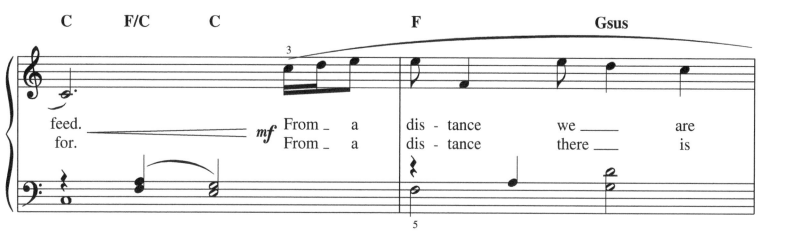

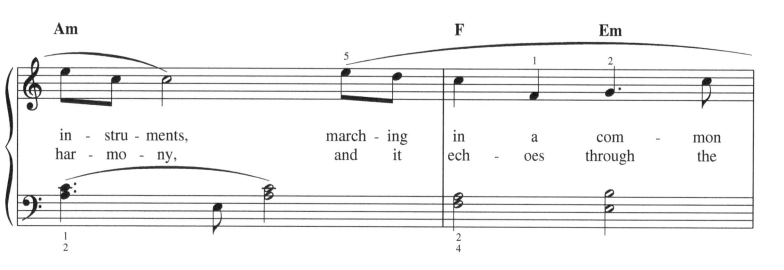

band. _____ Playing songs of hope, ___ playing
land. _____ It's the hope of hopes, ___ it's the

To Coda ⊕

songs of peace, ___ they're the songs of ev - 'ry
love of loves, ___ it's the heart of ev - 'ry

man. God __ is watch - ing us, ____ God __ is

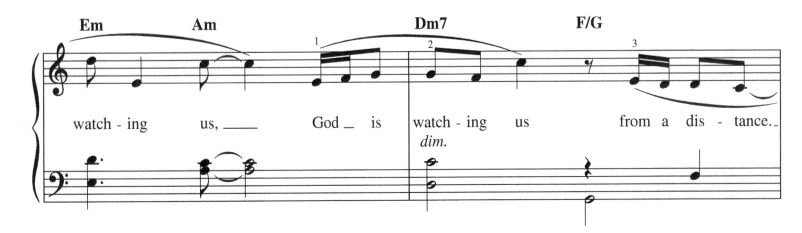

watch - ing us, ____ God __ is watch - ing us from a dis - tance. __
dim.

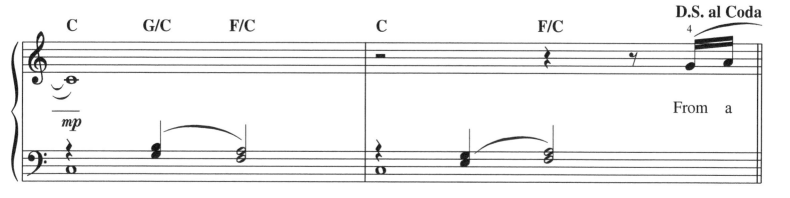

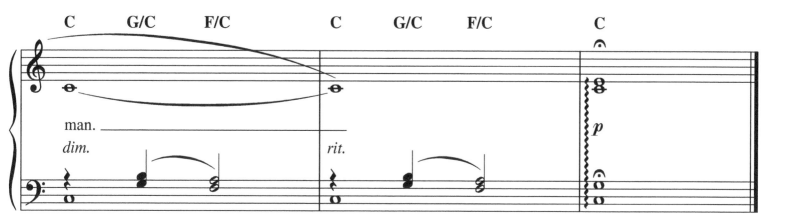

GOOD VIBRATIONS

Words and Music by BRIAN WILSON
and MIKE LOVE
Arranged by Phillip Keveren

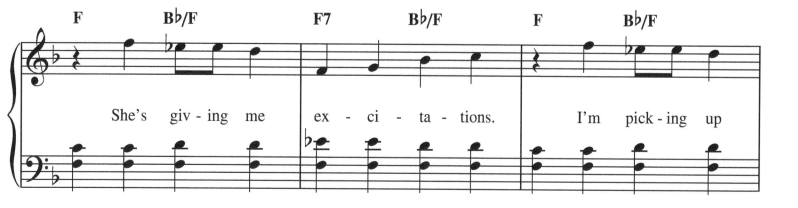

22

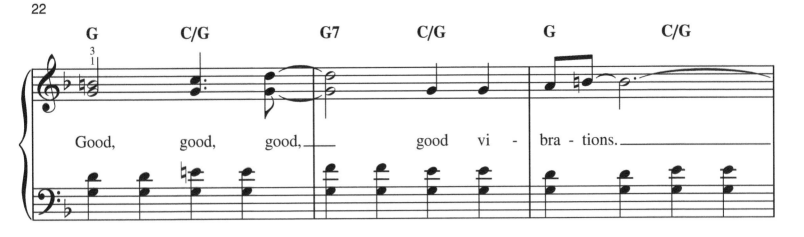

Good, good, good,___ good vi - bra - tions.___

___ Good, good, good,___ good vi -

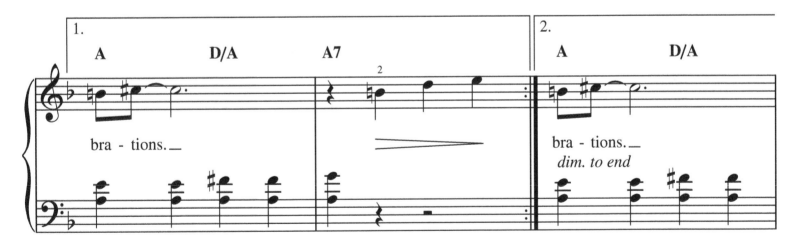

1.

bra - tions.___

2.

bra - tions.___
dim. to end

Good vi - bra - tions.___ Good vi - bra - tions.___

p

LET IT BE

Words and Music by JOHN LENNON
and PAUL McCARTNEY
Arranged by Phillip Keveren

Slowly (♩ = 60)

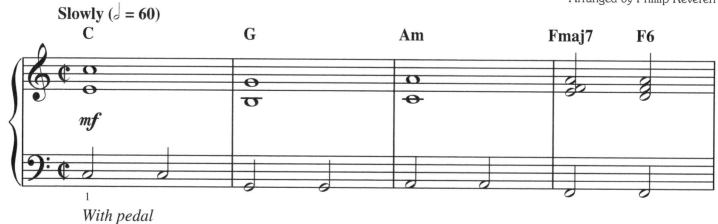

With pedal

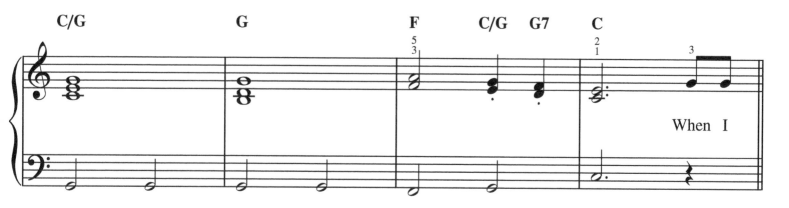

When I

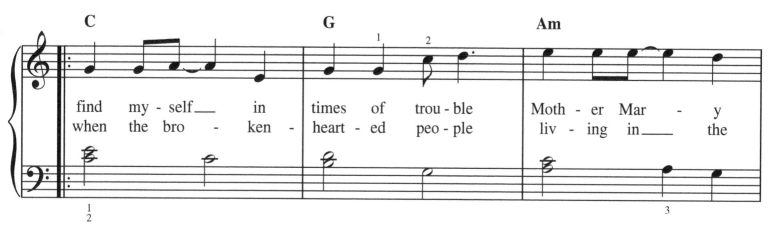

find my-self___ in times of trou-ble
when the bro-ken-heart-ed peo-ple

Moth-er Mar-y
liv-ing in___ the

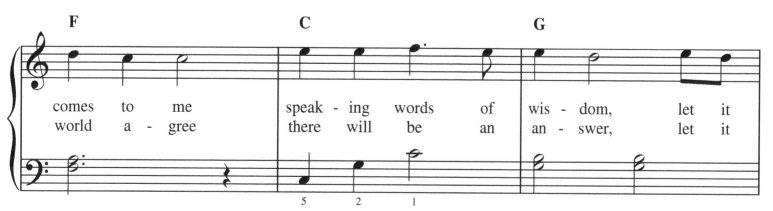

comes to me
world a-gree

speak-ing words of
there will be an

wis-dom, let it
an-swer, let it

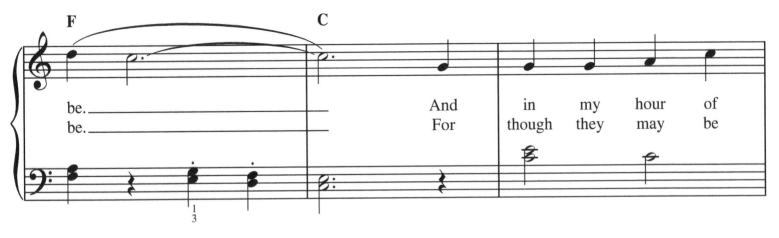

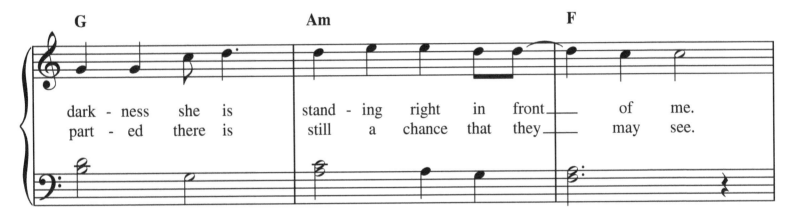

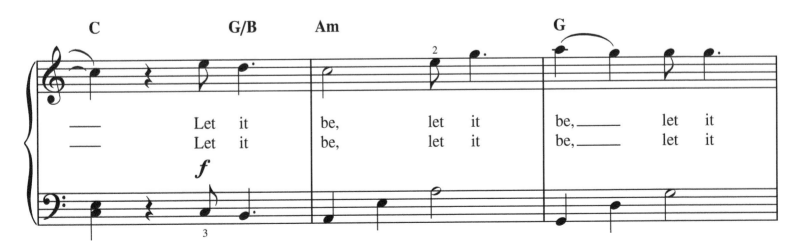

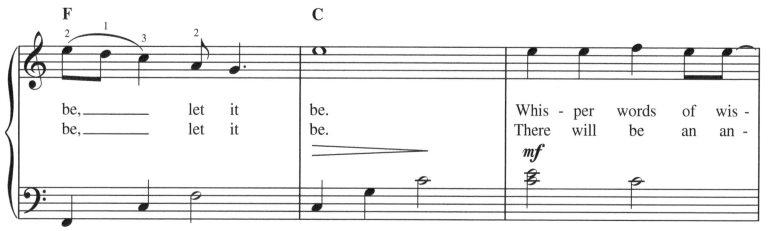

be,＿＿＿ let it be. Whis - per words of wis -
be,＿＿＿ let it be. There will be an an -

mf

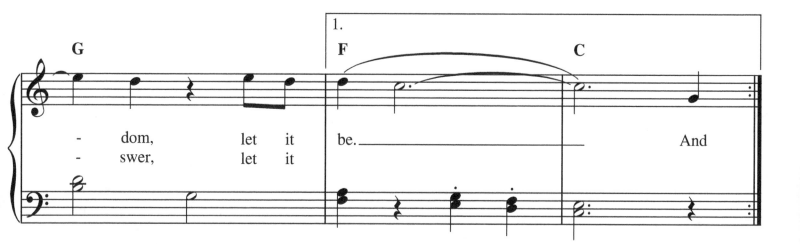

1.

- dom, let it be.＿＿＿ And
- swer, let it be.

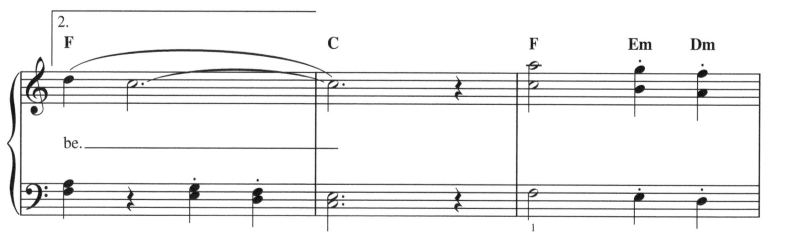

2.

be.＿＿＿

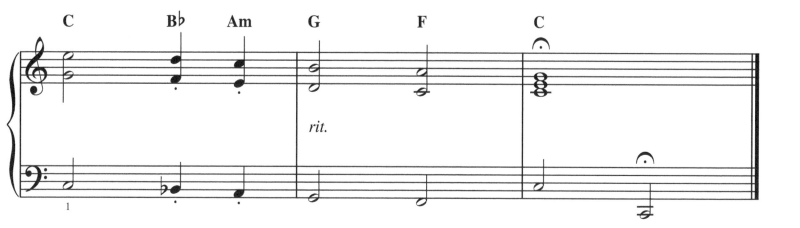

rit.

IMAGINE

Words and Music by
JOHN LENNON
Arranged by Phillip Keveren

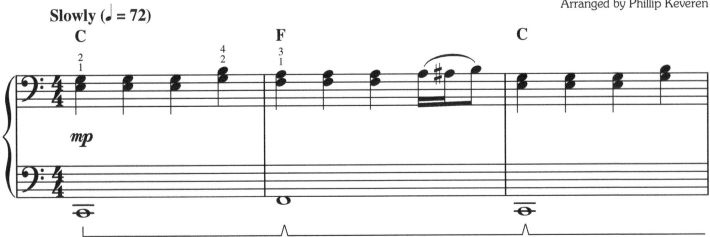

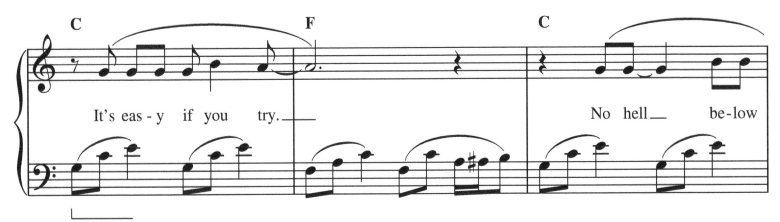

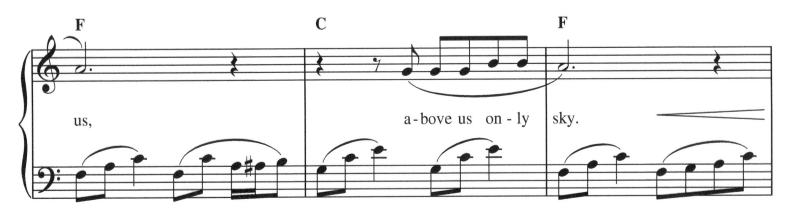

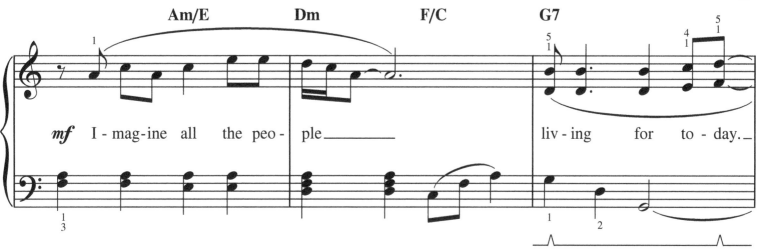

Am/E   Dm   F/C   G7

mf I - mag-ine all   the peo - ple_____   liv - ing   for   to - day.__

C   F

__ Ah._____   I - mag-ine there's   no coun - tries.

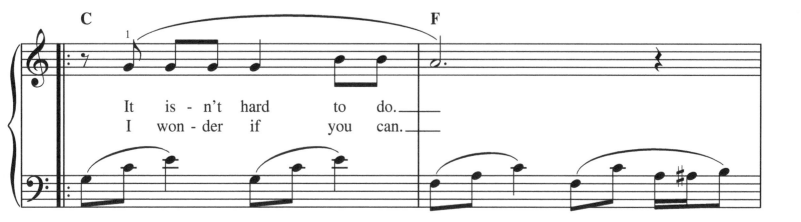

C   F

It is - n't hard   to   do.__
I   won - der if   you   can.__

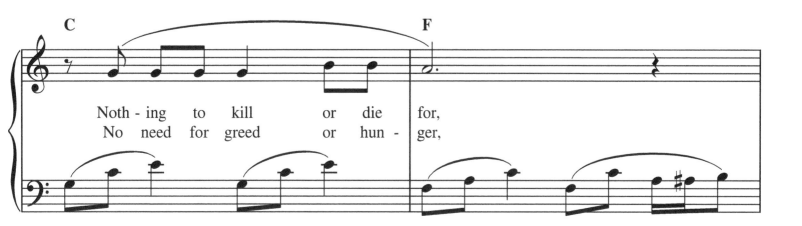

C   F

Noth - ing to kill   or   die   for,
No   need for greed   or   hun - ger,

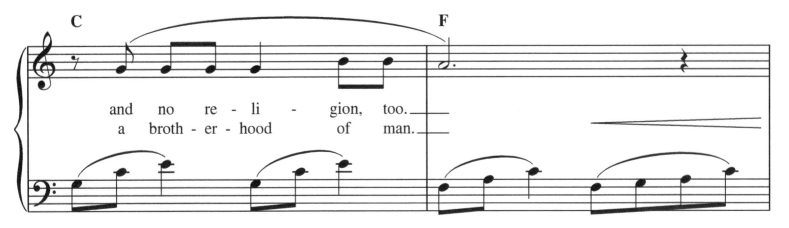

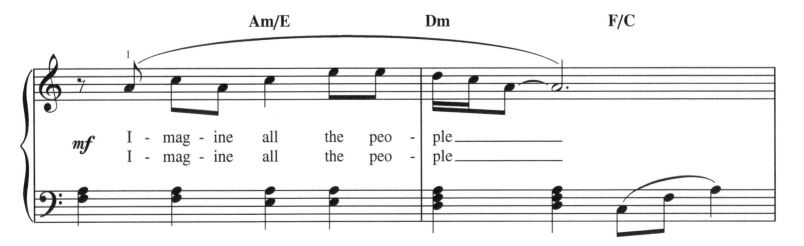

one. I hope some-day you'll_ join us

and the world will live as one.___ *mp*

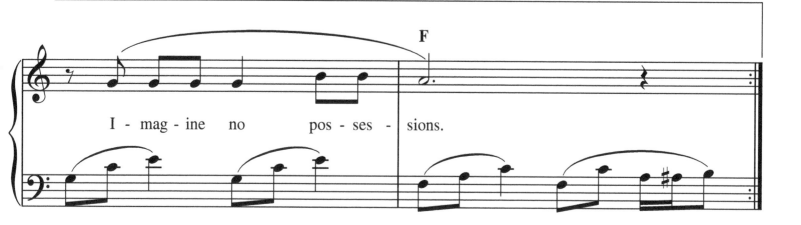

I - mag - ine no pos - ses - sions.

and the world will_ live as one.
dim. e rit. *p*

MANDY

Words and Music by SCOTT ENGLISH
and RICHARD KERR
Arranged by Phillip Keveren

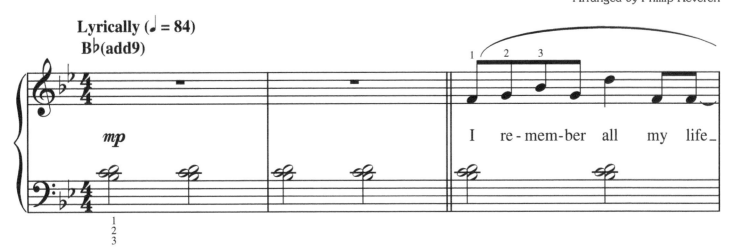

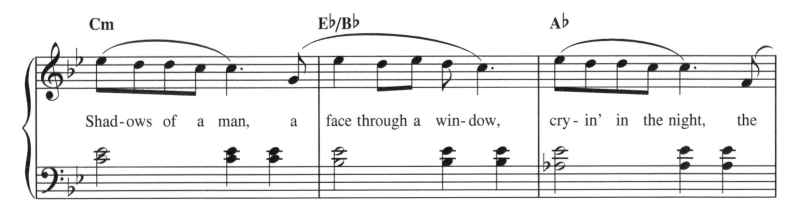

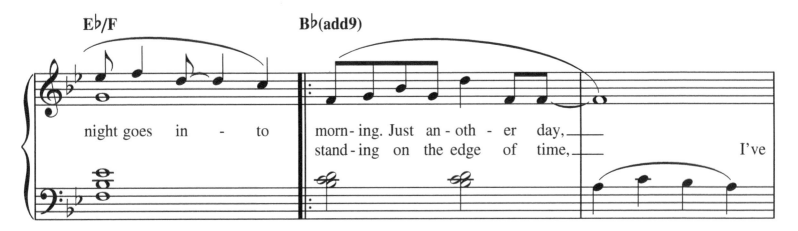

hap - py peo - ple pass my way.___
walked a - way when love was mine.___

Look - ing in their eyes, I
Caught up in a world of

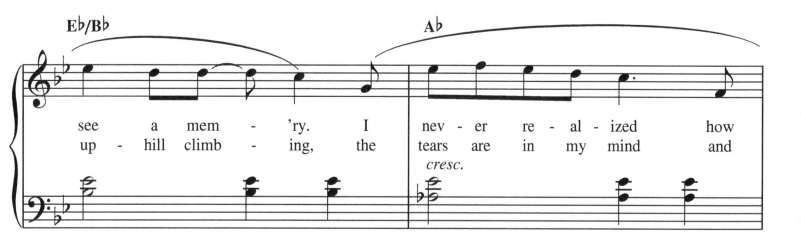

see a mem - 'ry. I
up - hill climb - ing, the

nev - er re - al - ized how
tears are in my mind how and

cresc.

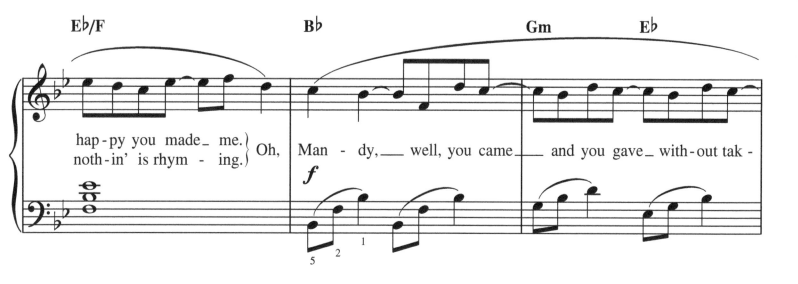

hap - py you made_ me.
noth - in' is rhym - ing.

Oh, Man - dy,___ well, you came___ and you gave_ with - out tak -

f

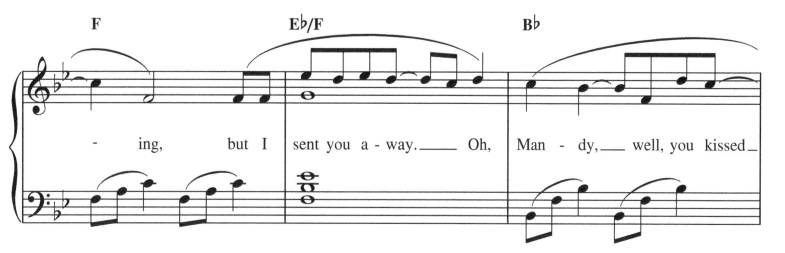

- ing, but I sent you a - way.___ Oh, Man - dy,___ well, you kissed_

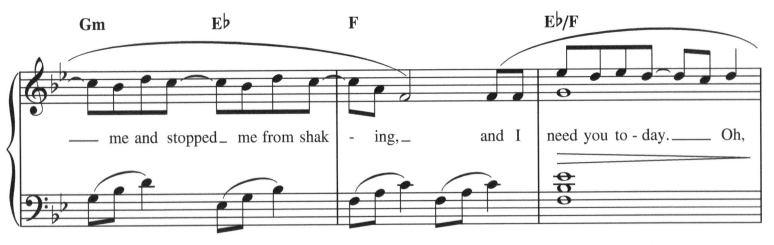

Gm   E♭   F   E♭/F

— me and stopped — me from shak - ing, — and I need you to - day. ——— Oh,

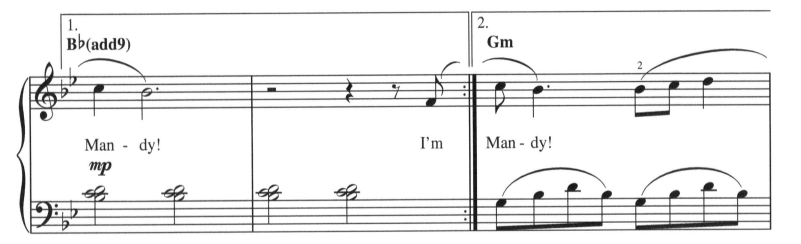

1.
B♭(add9)

mp

Man - dy!   I'm

2.
Gm

Man - dy!

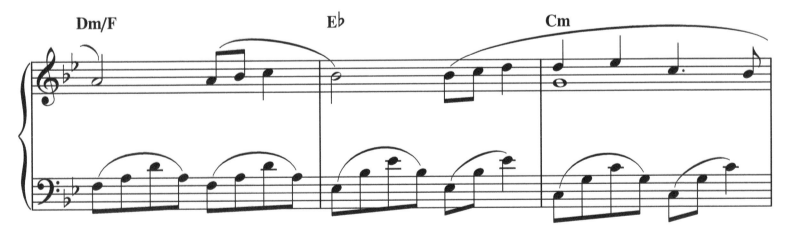

Dm/F   E♭   Cm

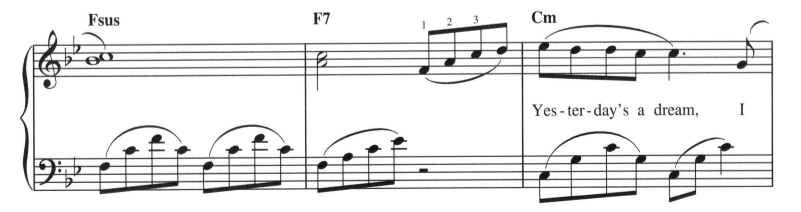

Fsus   F7   Cm

Yes - ter - day's a dream,   I

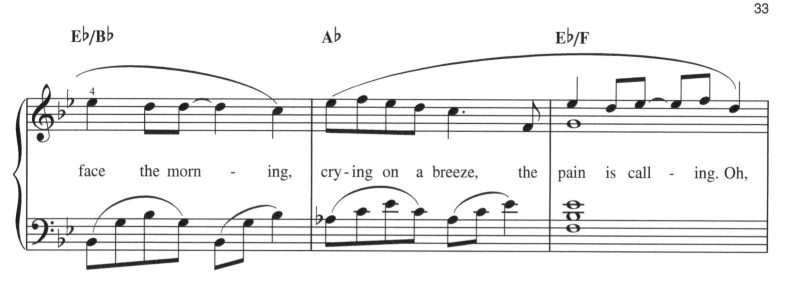

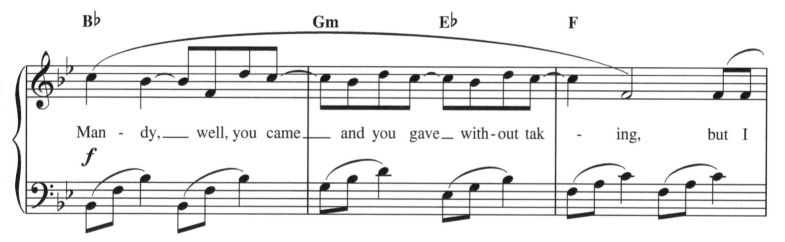

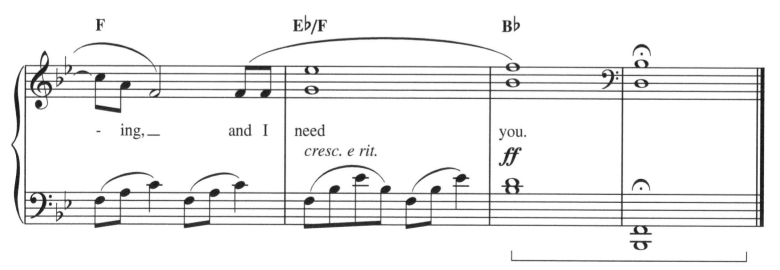

NEW YORK STATE OF MIND

Words and Music by
BILLY JOEL
Arranged by Phillip Keveren

Slow and bluesy (♩ = 60)

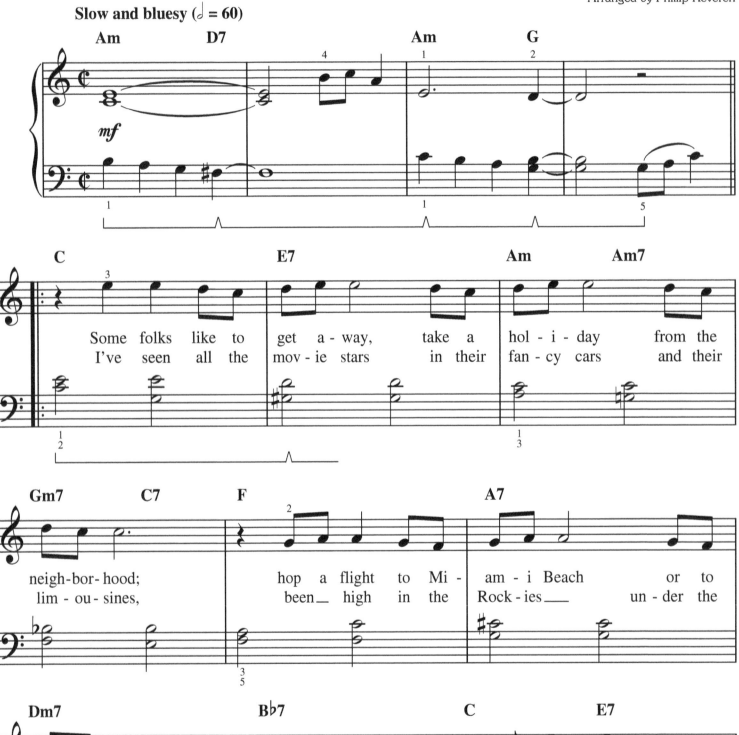

Some folks like to get a - way, take a hol - i - day from the
I've seen all the mov - ie stars in their fan - cy cars and their

neigh - bor - hood; hop a flight to Mi - am - i Beach or to
lim - ou - sines, been_ high in the Rock - ies___ un - der the

Hol - ly - wood._____ But I'm tak - in' a
ev - er - greens._____ But I know what I'm

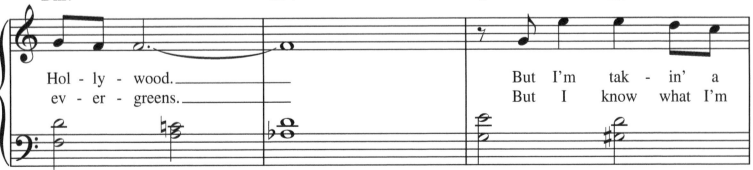

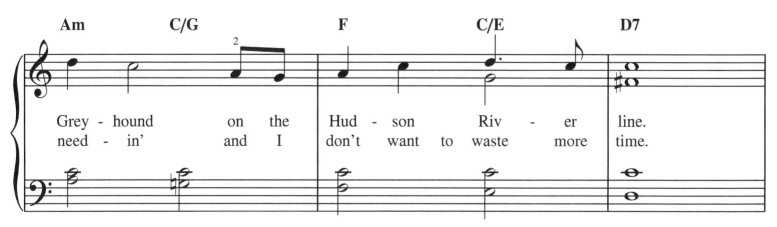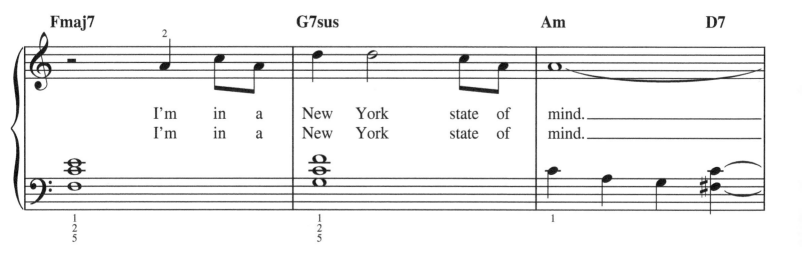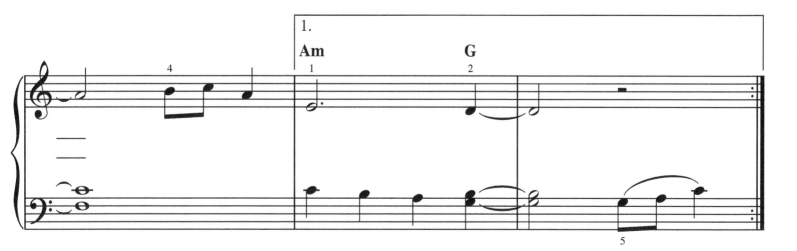

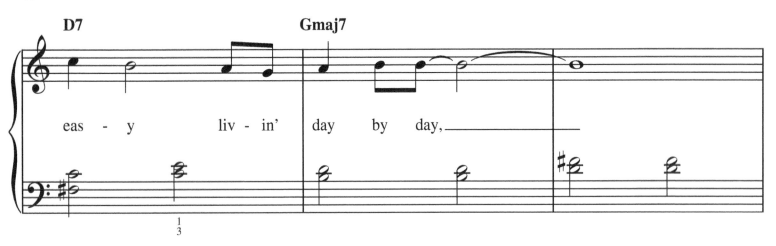

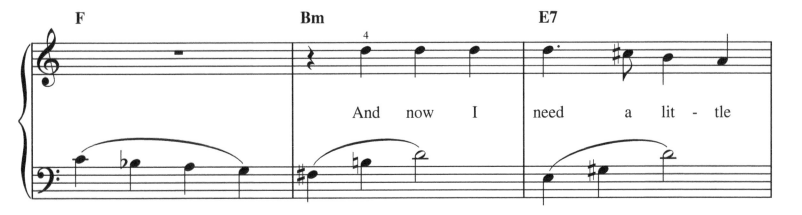

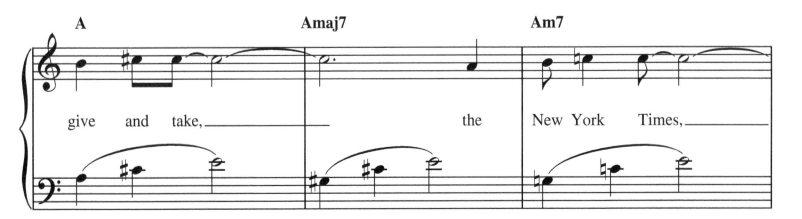

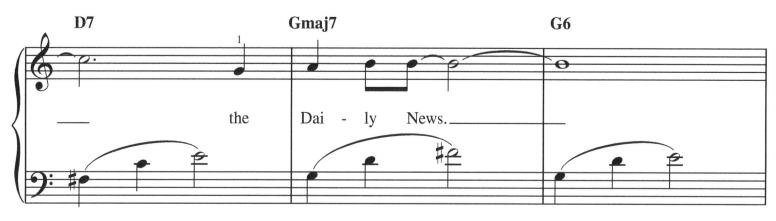

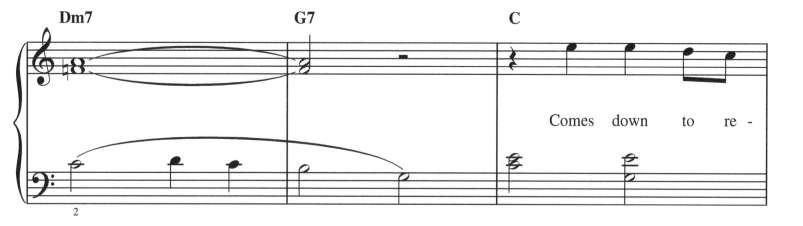

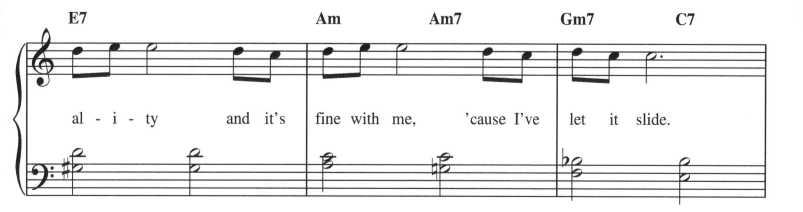

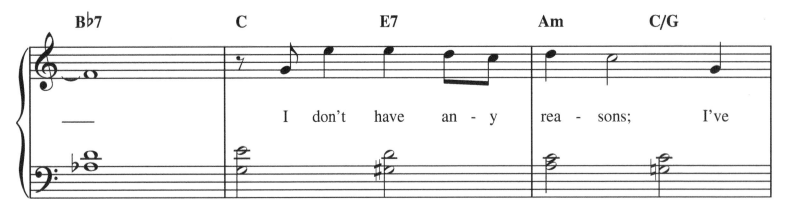

I don't have an - y rea - sons; I've

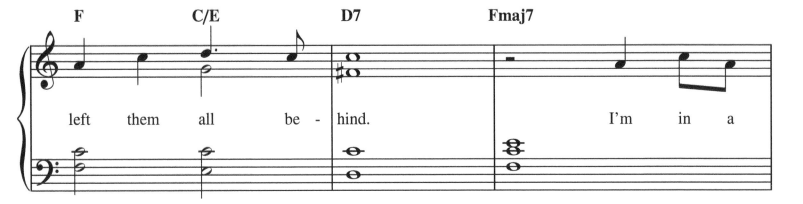

left them all be - hind. I'm in a

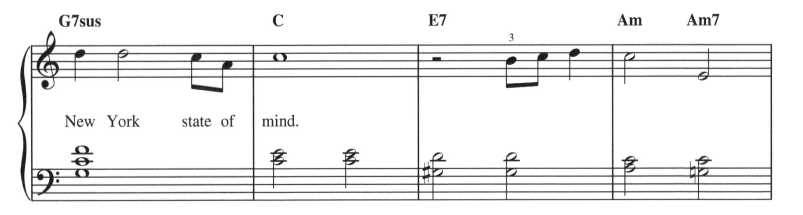

New York state of mind.

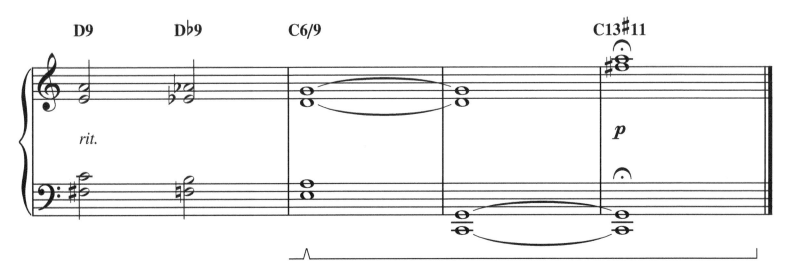

RAINY DAYS AND MONDAYS

Lyrics by PAUL WILLIAMS
Music by ROGER NICHOLS
Arranged by Phillip Keveren

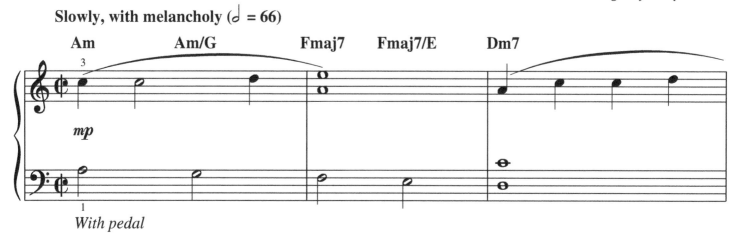

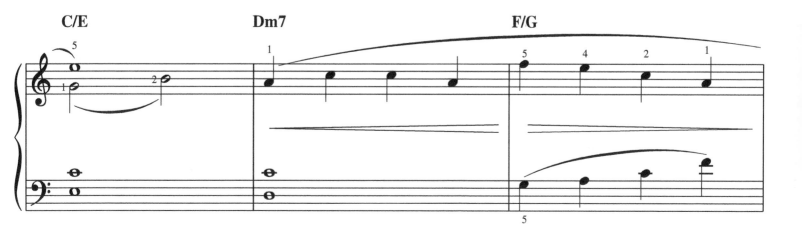

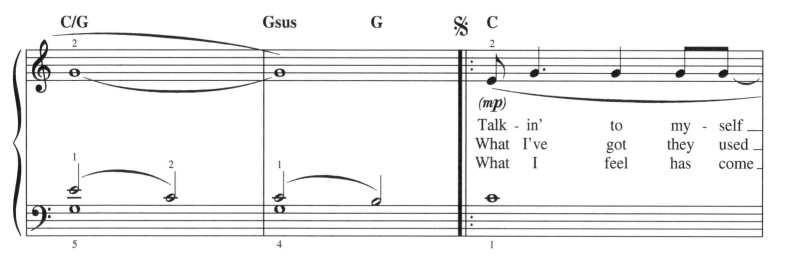

Talk - in' to my - self
What I've got they used
What I feel has come

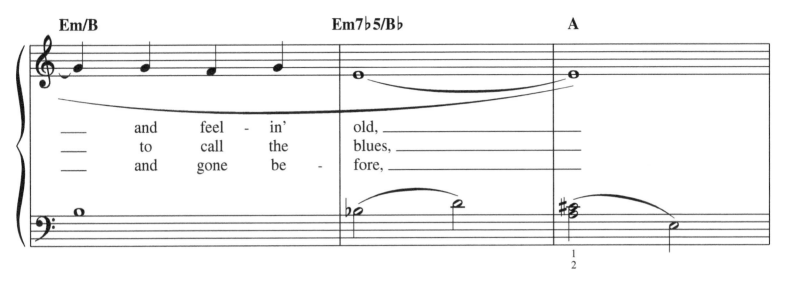

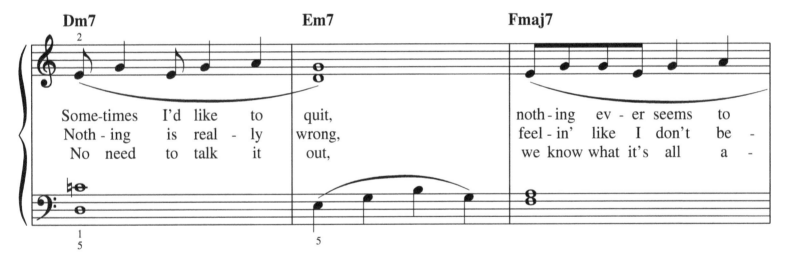

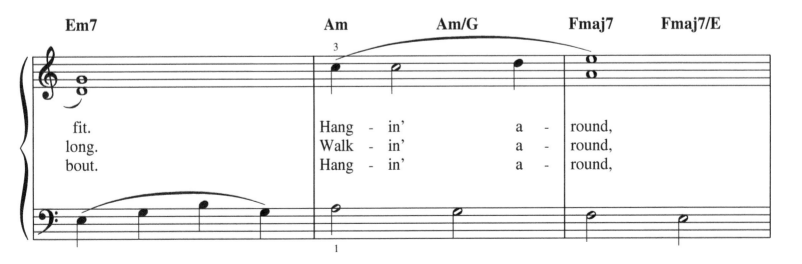

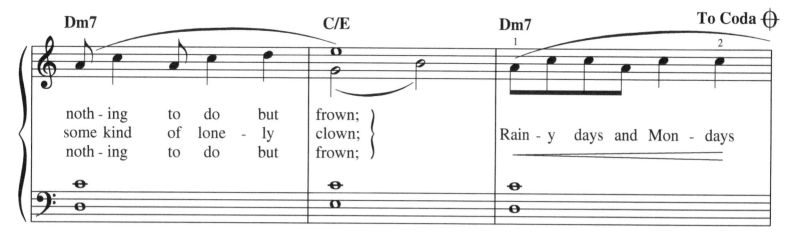

Dm7 · C/E · Dm7 · To Coda

noth - ing to do but frown;
some kind of lone - ly clown;
noth - ing to do but frown;

Rain - y days and Mon - days

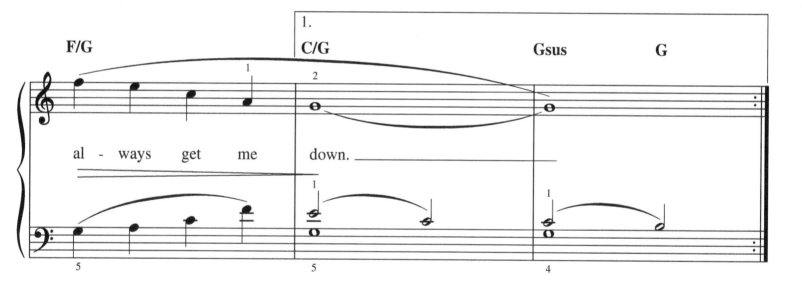

F/G · C/G · Gsus · G

al - ways get me down.

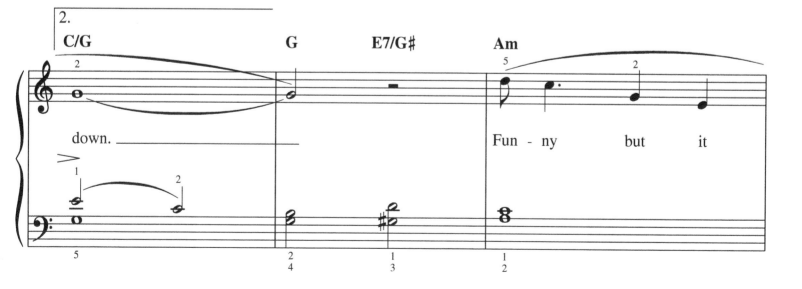

2.
C/G · G · E7/G♯ · Am

down.

Fun - ny but it

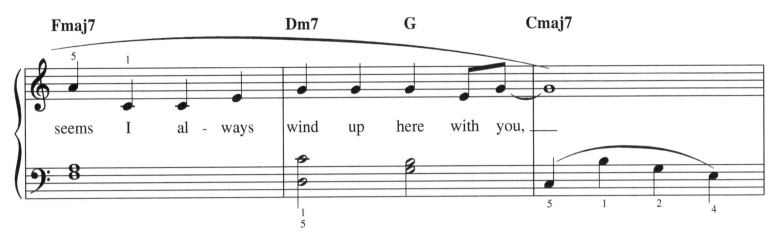

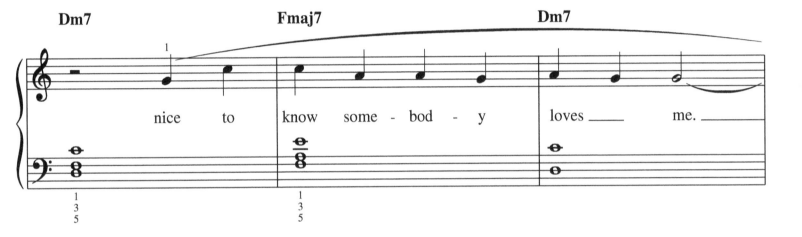

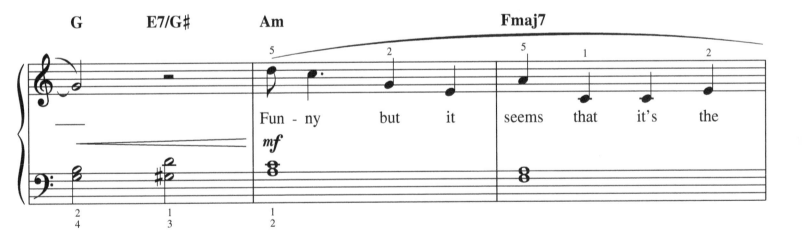

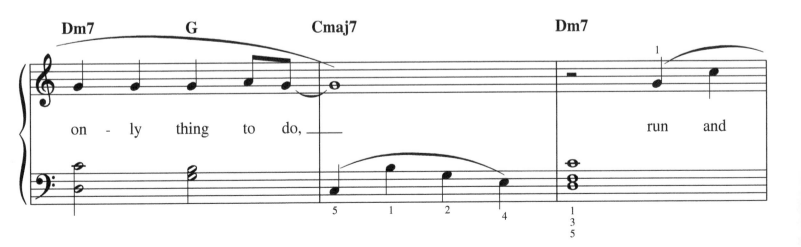

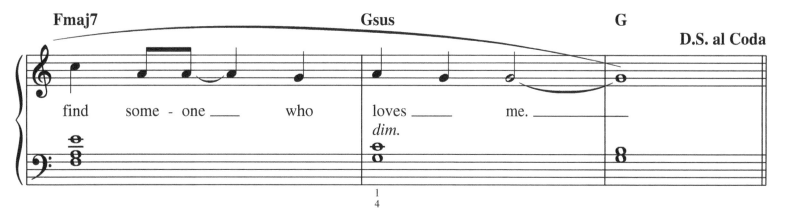

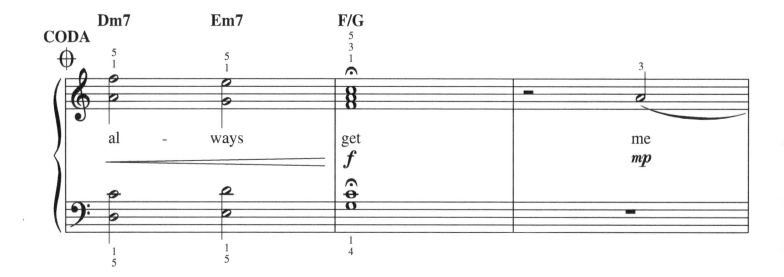

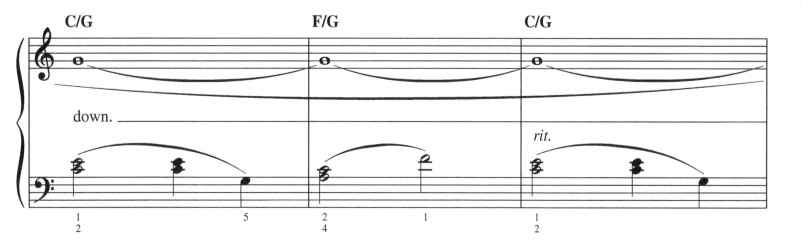

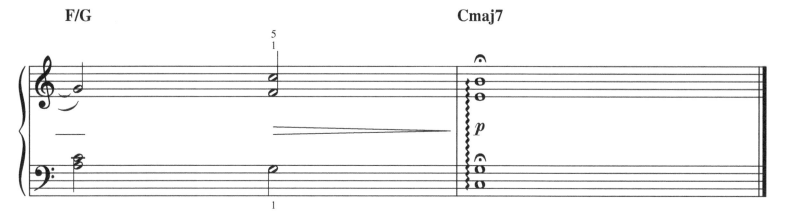

SHE'S GOT A WAY

Words and Music by
BILLY JOEL
Arranged by Phillip Keveren

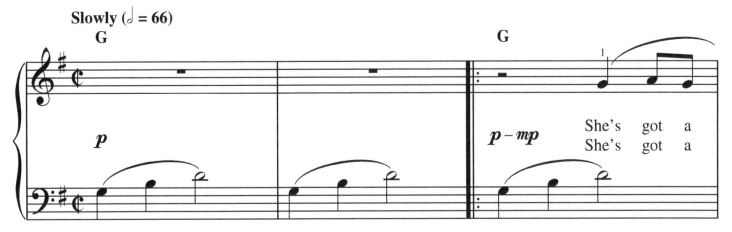

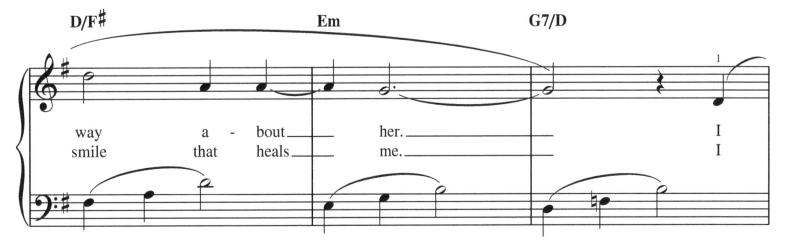

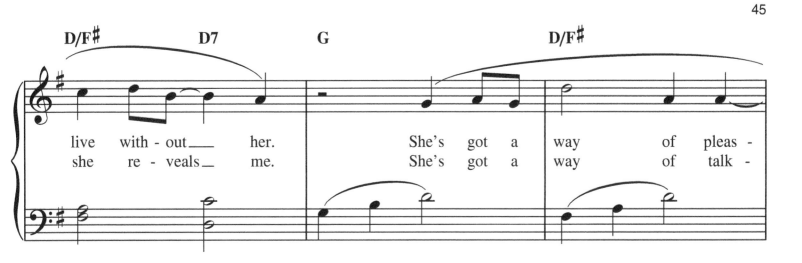

live with - out___ her. She's got a way of pleas -
she re - veals__ me. She's got a way of talk -

\- in'.___ I don't know why it is,___
\- in'.___ I don't know why it is,___

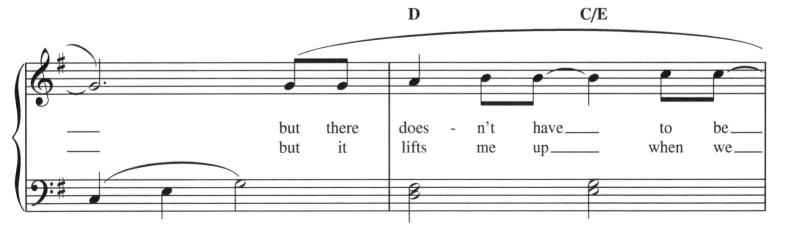

___ but there does - n't have___ to be___
___ but it lifts me up___ when we___

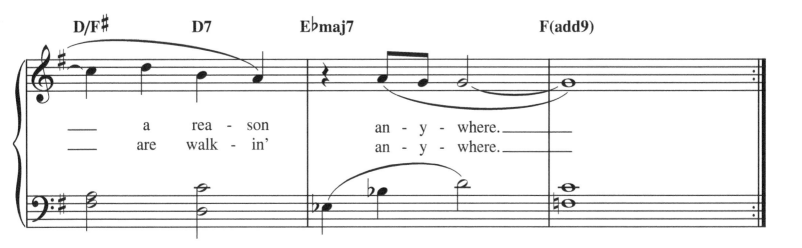

___ a rea - son an - y - where.___
___ are walk - in' an - y - where.___

G   D

She comes to me____ when I'm

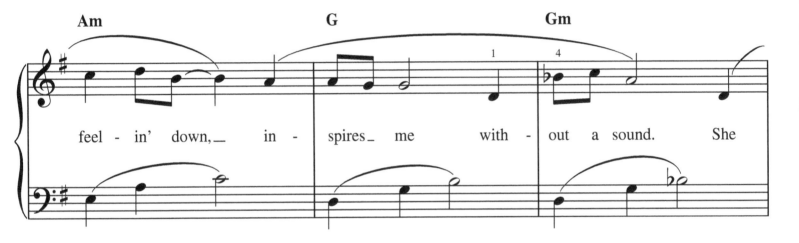

Am   G   Gm

feel - in' down,___ in - spires__ me with - out a sound. She

D/F#   F#   F#/A#   Bm

touch - es me and I get turned a - round.____

D7   G   D/F#

To Coda

mf   She's got a way of show -

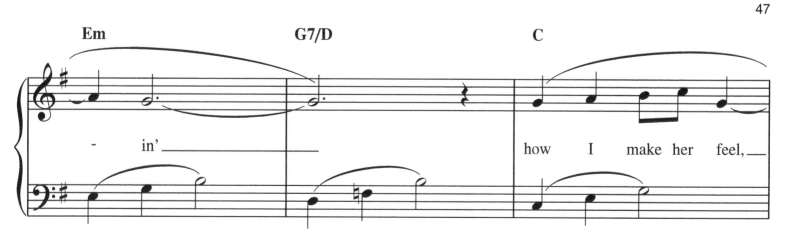

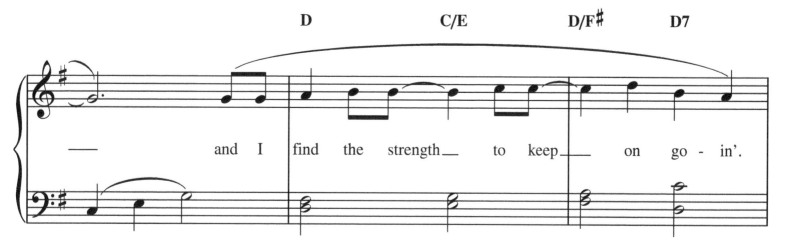

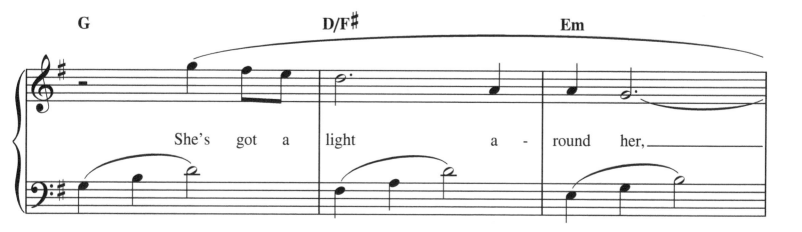

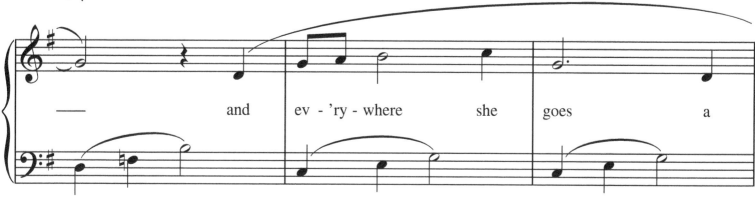

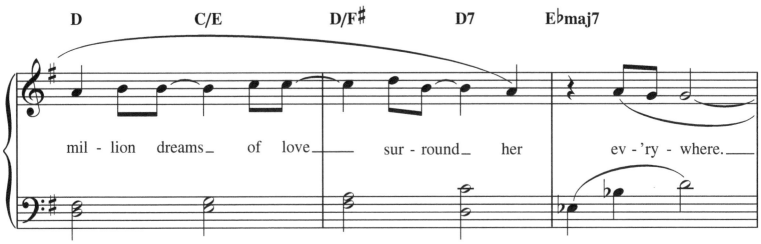

D   **C/E**   **D/F♯**   **D7**   **E♭maj7**

mil - lion dreams___ of love___ sur - round___ her ev - 'ry - where.___

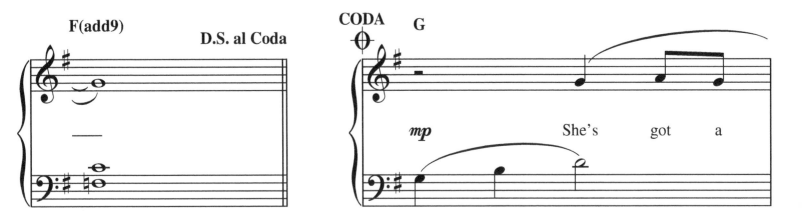

F(add9)   **D.S. al Coda**   **CODA**   **G**

mp   She's got a

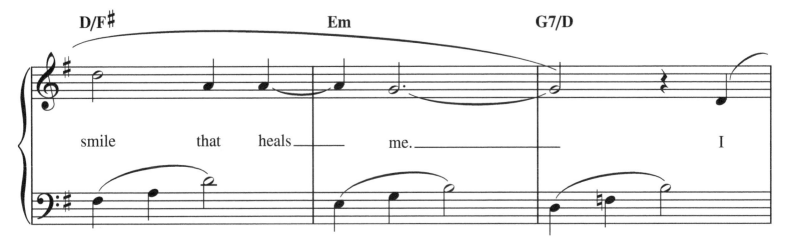

D/F♯   **Em**   **G7/D**

smile that heals___ me.___ I

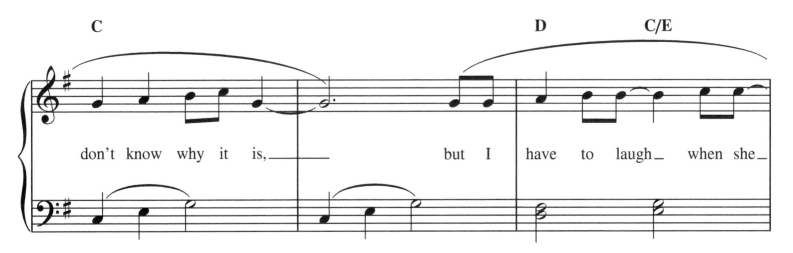

C   **D**   **C/E**

don't know why it is,___ but I have to laugh___ when she___

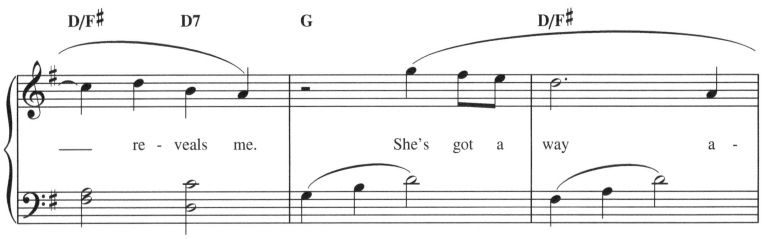

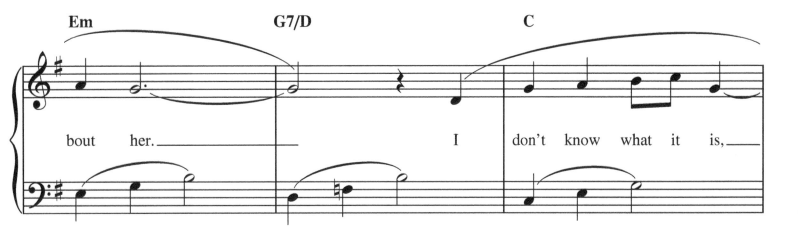

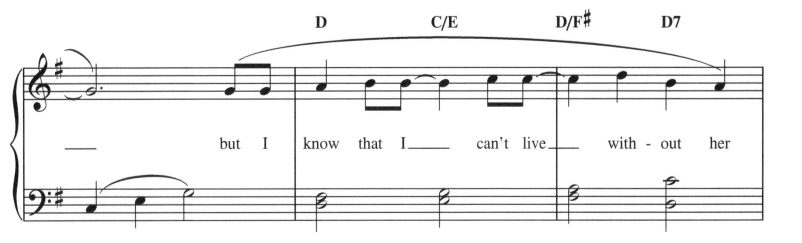

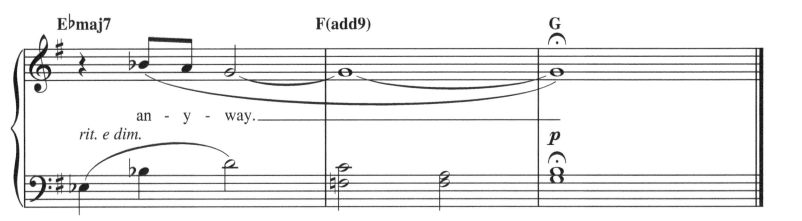

SIR DUKE

Words and Music by
STEVIE WONDER
Arranged by Phillip Keveren

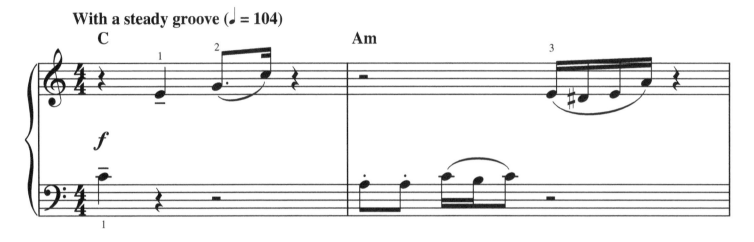

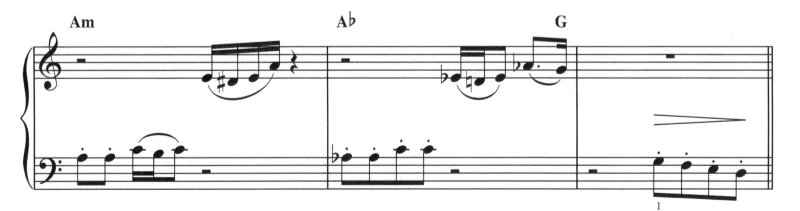

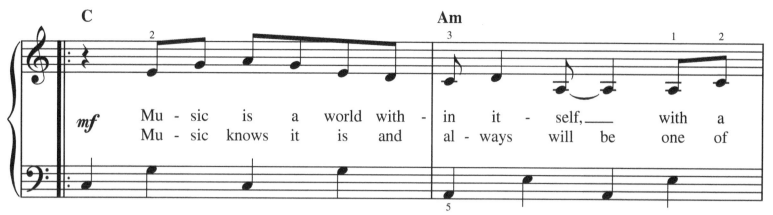

C ... **Am**

Mu - sic is a world with - in it - self,____ with a
Mu - sic knows it is and al - ways will be one of

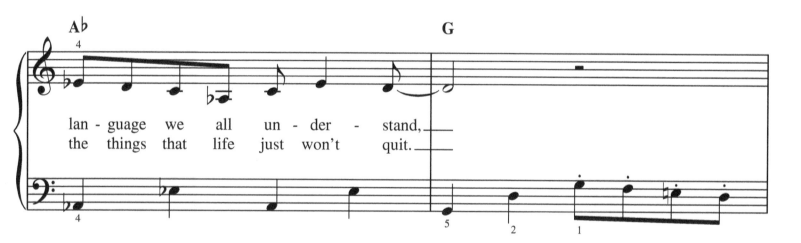

A♭ ... **G**

lan - guage we all un - der - stand,____
the things that life just won't quit.____

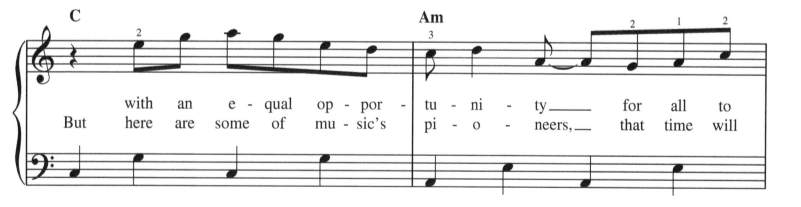

C ... **Am**

with an e - qual op - por - tu - ni - ty____ for all to
But here are some of mu - sic's pi - o - neers,____ that time will

A♭ ... **G**

sing,____ dance and clap their hands.____
not al - low us to for - get:____

But just be -
For there's

mp

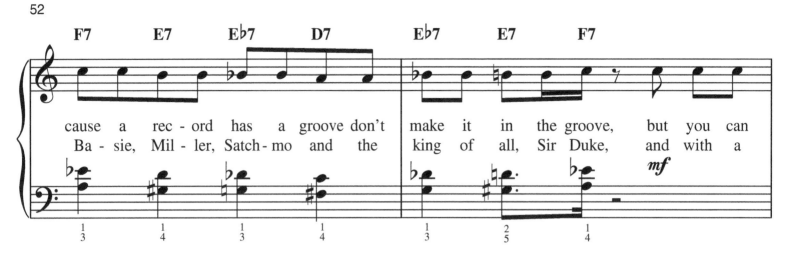

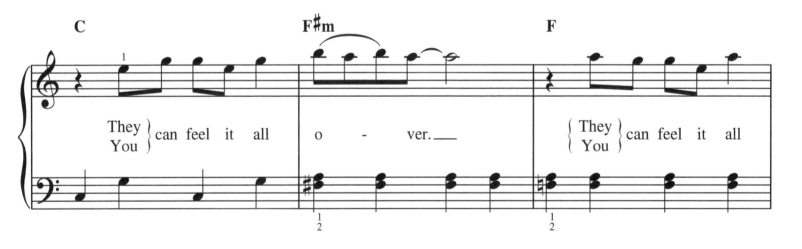

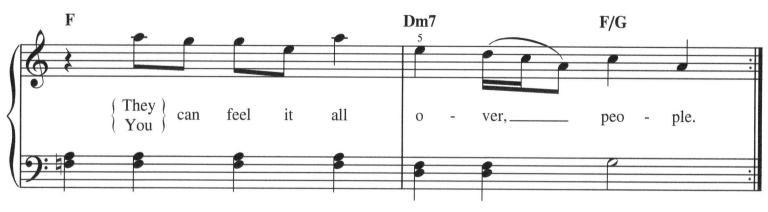

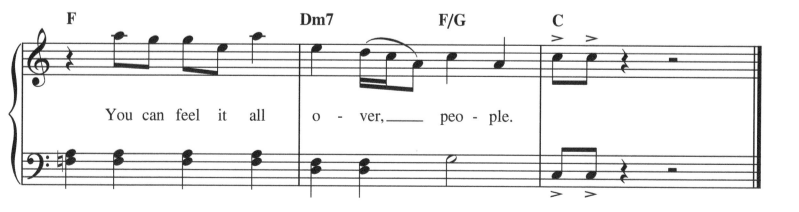

SO FAR AWAY

Words and Music by
CAROLE KING
Arranged by Phillip Keveren

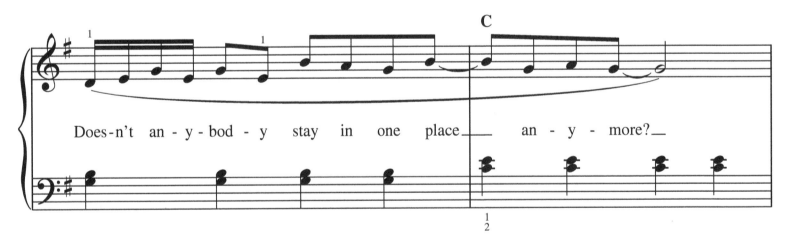

Does - n't help to know you're just time a - way.

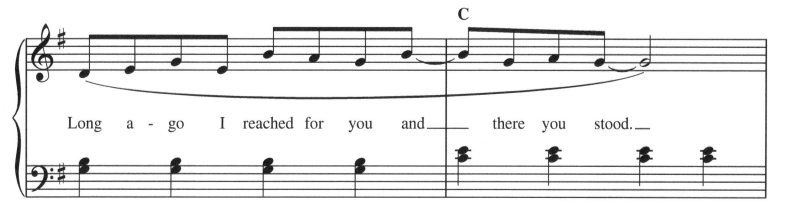

Long a - go I reached for you and____ there you stood.____

Hold - ing you a - gain could on - ly do me____ good.____

How I wish____ I could, but you're so far a - way!

Bm/F#   Em   G/D

One more song a-bout mov-in' a-long the
mf

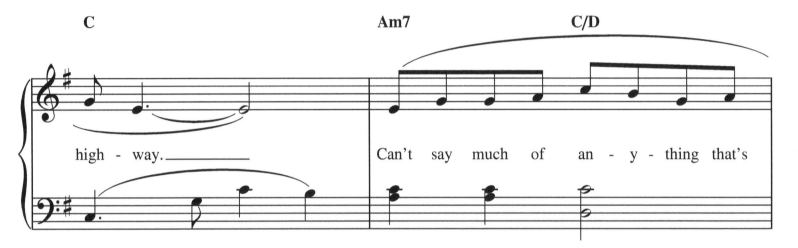

C   Am7   C/D

high - way._____ Can't say much of an - y - thing that's

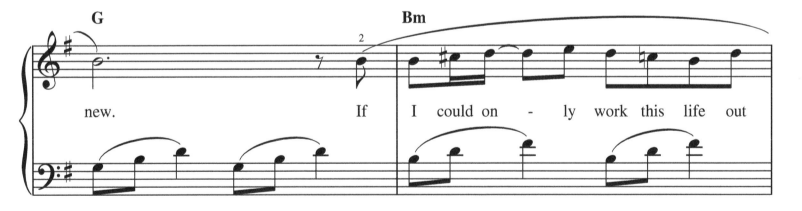

G   Bm

new.   If   I could on - ly work this life out

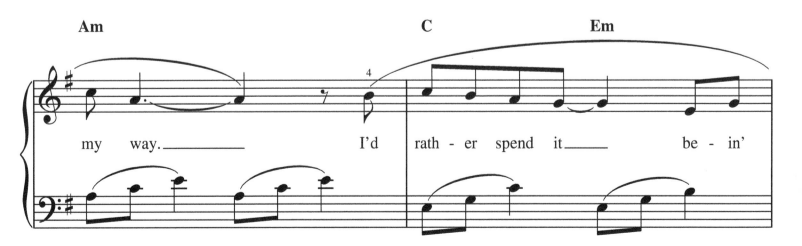

Am   C   Em

my way._____   I'd rath - er spend it_____ be - in'

close to you._____ But you're so far a - way.

mp

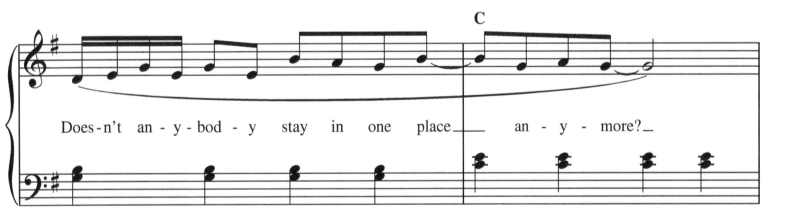

Does-n't an-y-bod-y stay in one place___ an-y-more?___

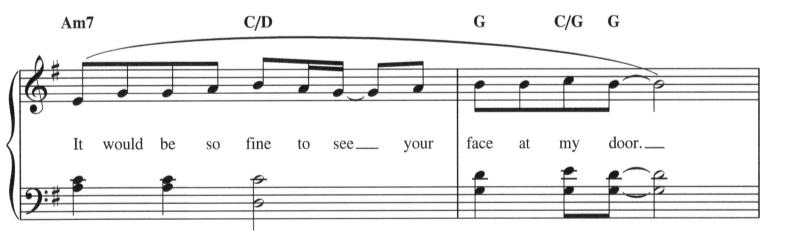

It would be so fine to see___ your face at my door.___

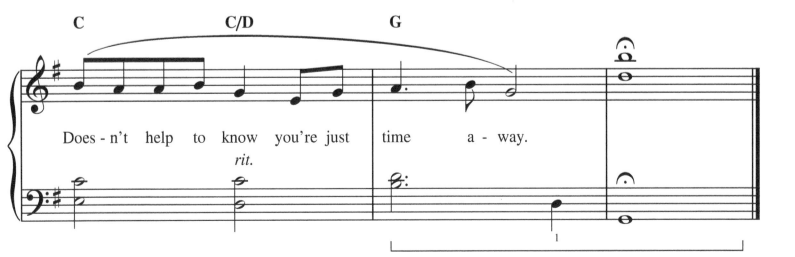

Does-n't help to know you're just time a - way.

rit.

1

SORRY SEEMS TO BE
THE HARDEST WORD

Words and Music by ELTON JOHN
and BERNIE TAUPIN
Arranged by Phillip Keveren

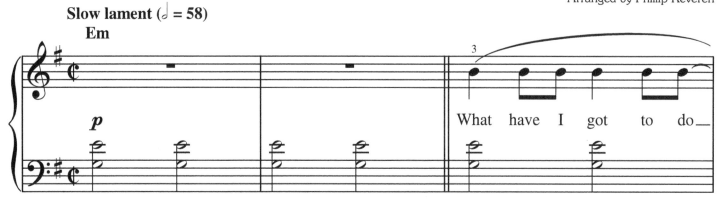

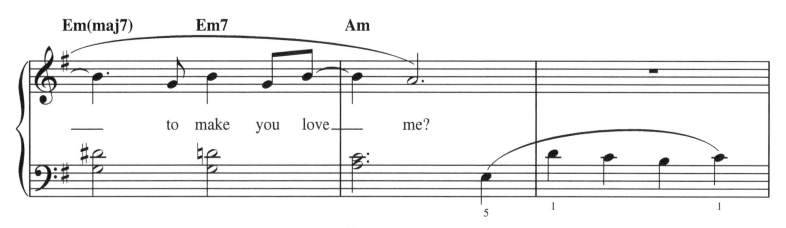

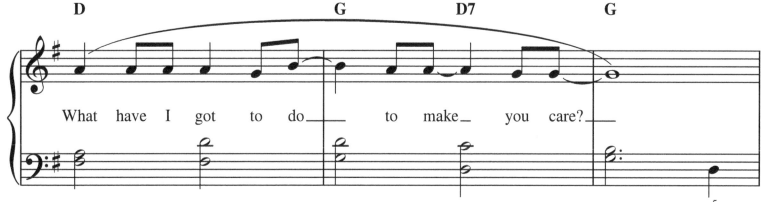

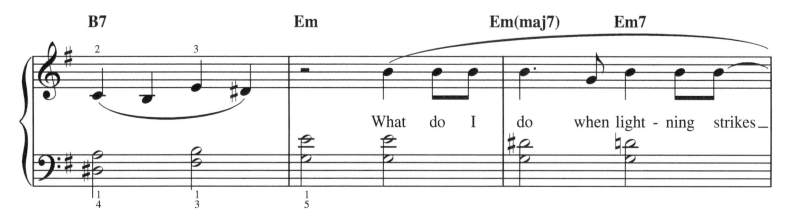

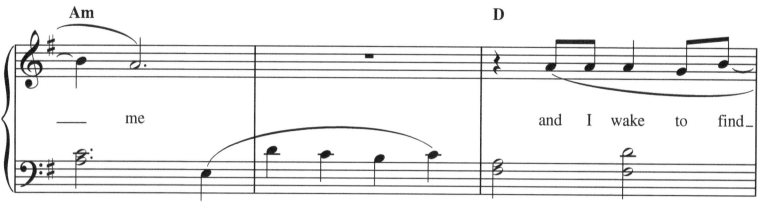

Am   D

me   and I wake to find

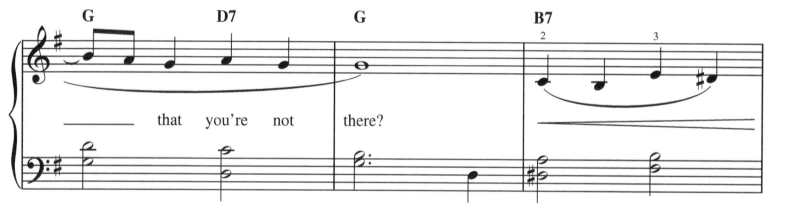

G   D7   G   B7

that you're not there?

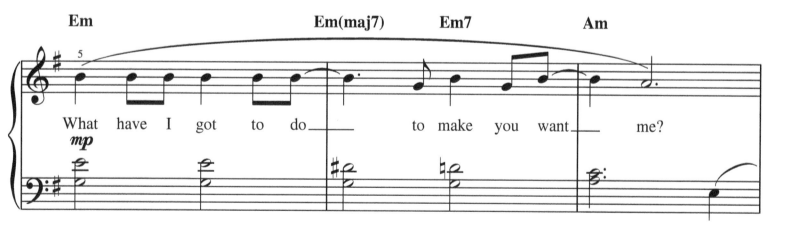

Em   Em(maj7)   Em7   Am

What have I got to do_____ to make you want_____ me?

mp

D   G   D7

What have I got to do_____ to be heard?_

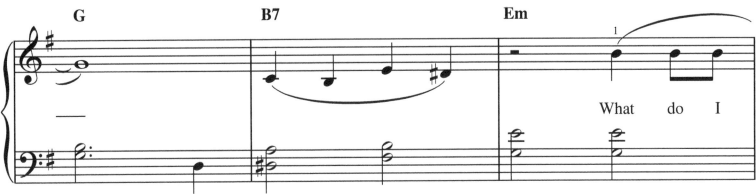

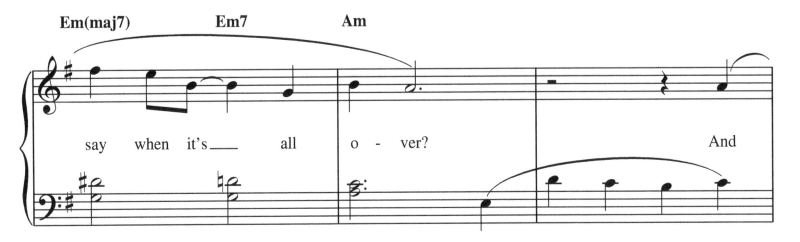

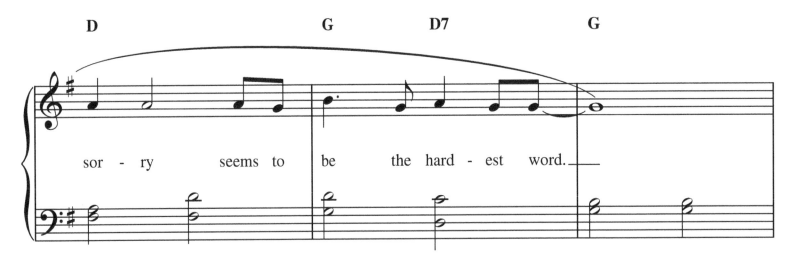

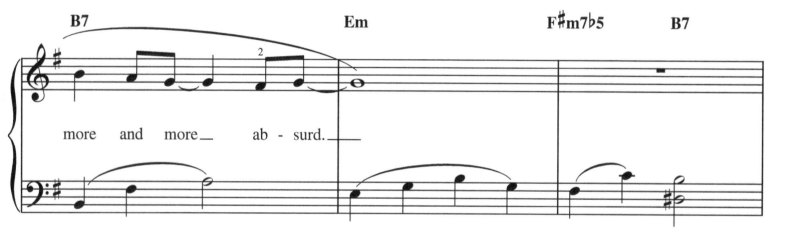

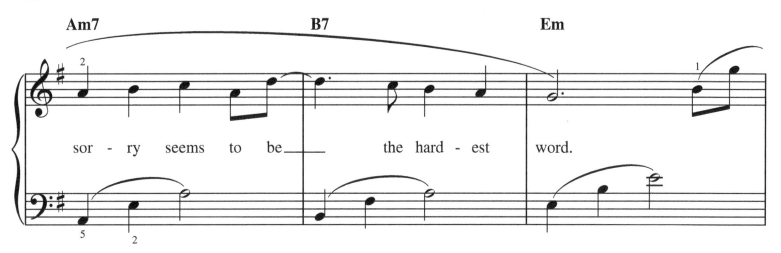

sor - ry seems to be ___ the hard - est word.

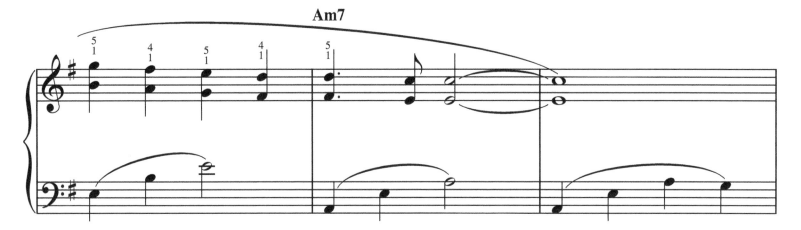

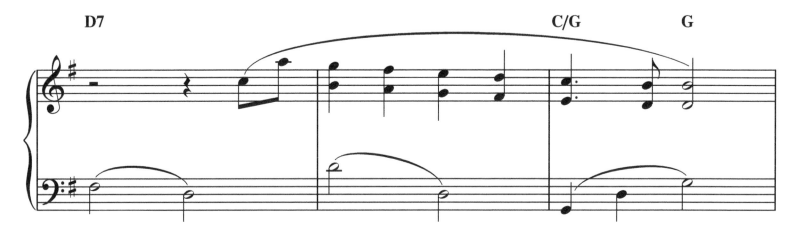

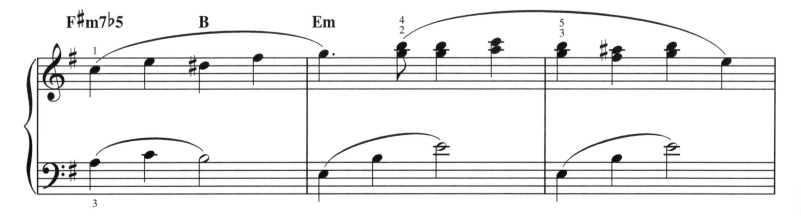

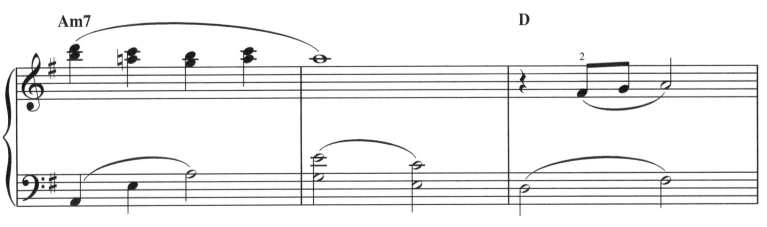

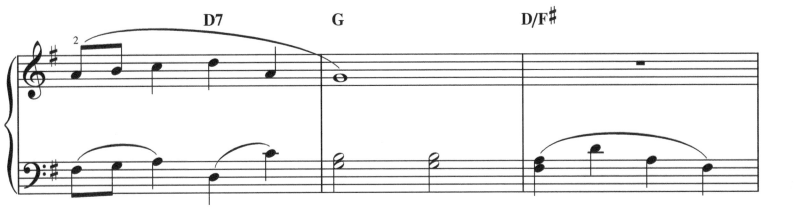

It's sad,_____ it's sad,_____ it's a sad, sad

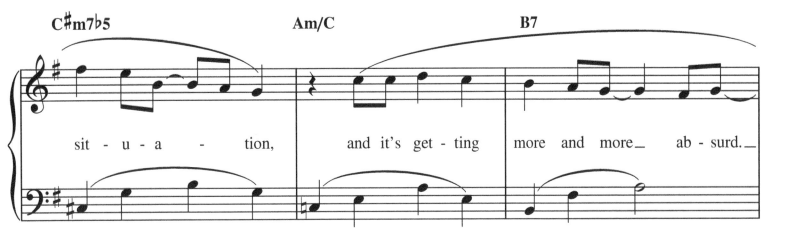

sit - u - a - tion, and it's get - ting more and more_ ab - surd._

Em   F#m7b5   B7   C/E

It's sad,_____

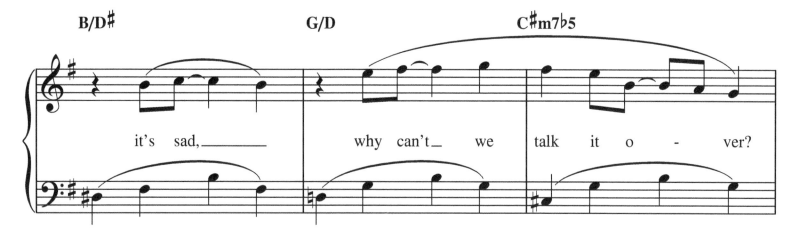

B/D#   G/D   C#m7b5

it's sad,_____   why can't__ we   talk it o - ver?

Am/C   Am7

Oh, it seems to me____   that   sor - ry seems to be__

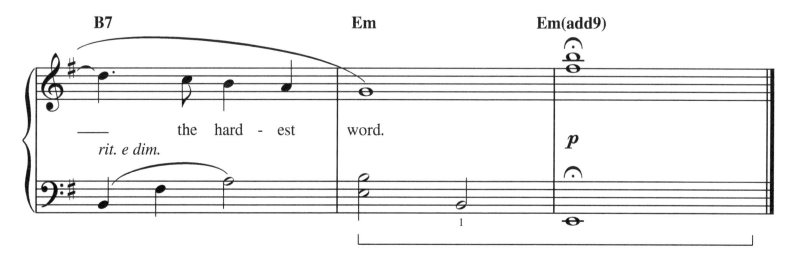

B7   Em   Em(add9)

__ the hard - est   word.

rit. e dim.

p

THREE TIMES A LADY

Words and Music by
LIONEL RICHIE
Arranged by Phillip Keveren

Gently (♩ = 84)

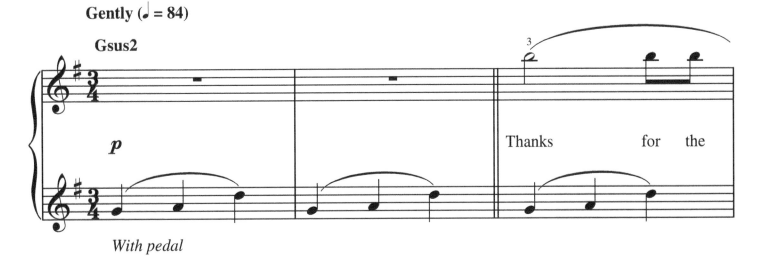

With pedal

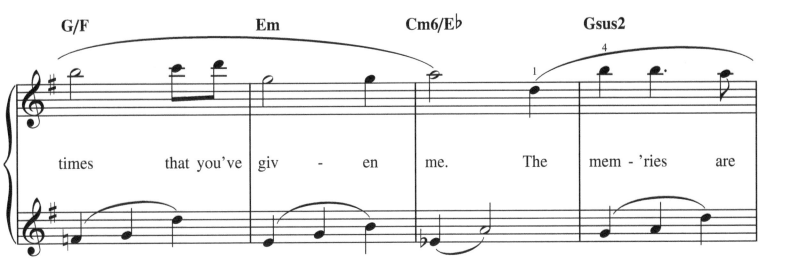

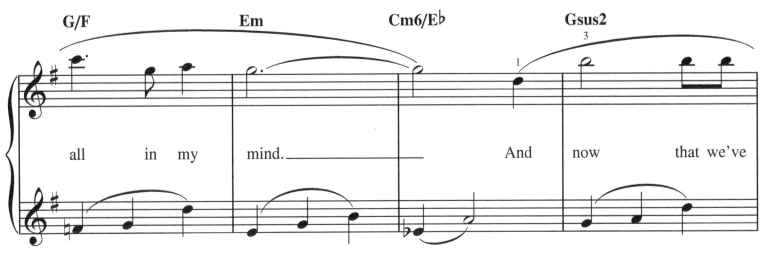

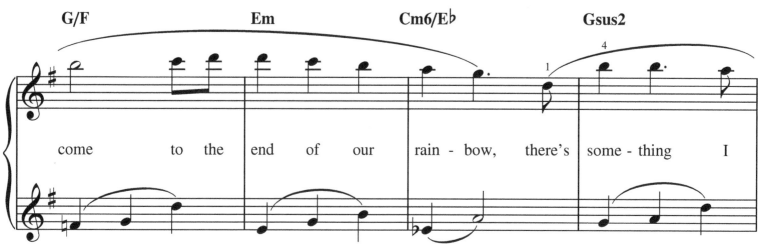

come to the end of our rain - bow, there's some - thing I

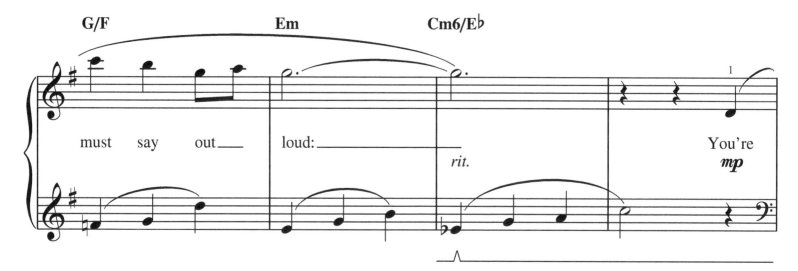

must say out___ loud:___ *rit.* You're ***mp***

once, *a tempo* twice, three times a la - dy,___

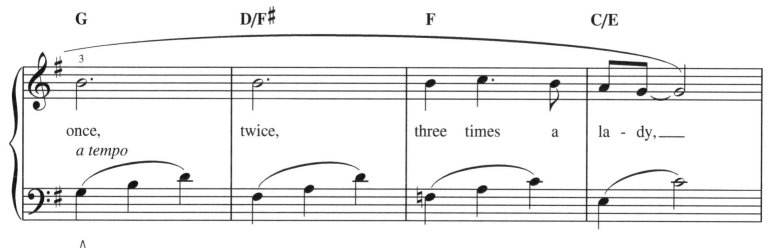

and I love___ you.___ Yes, you're

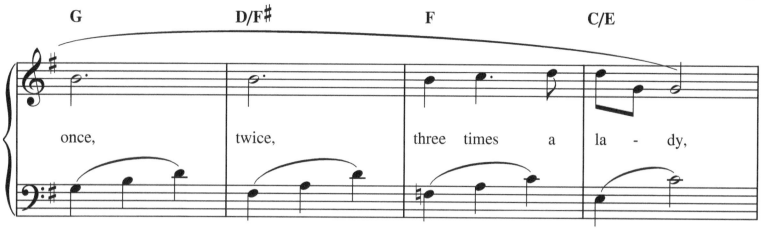

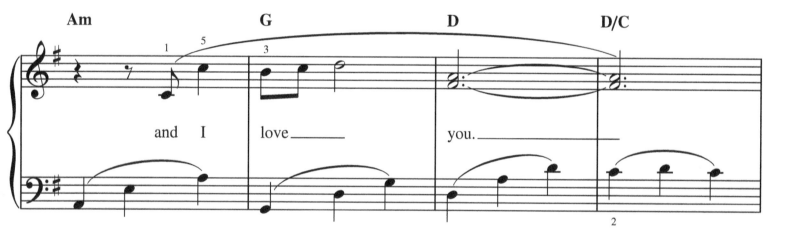

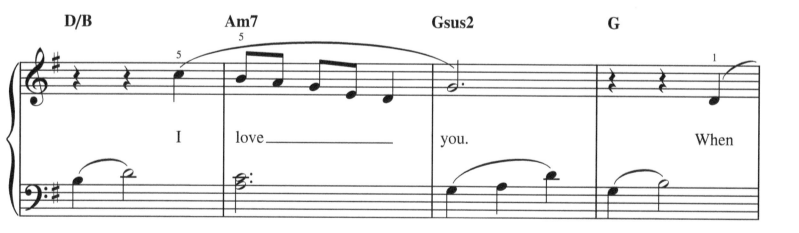

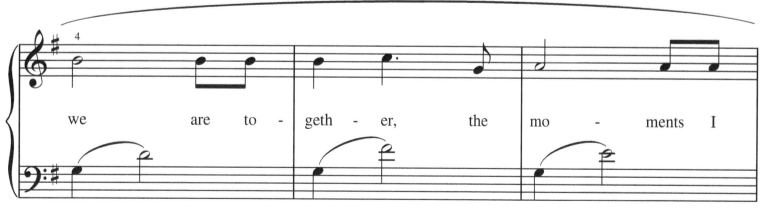

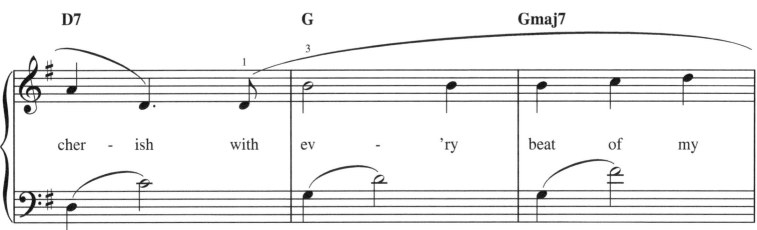

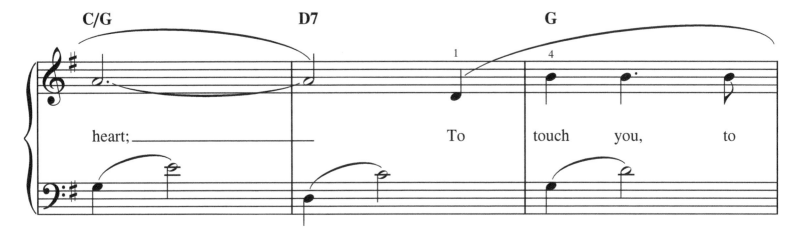

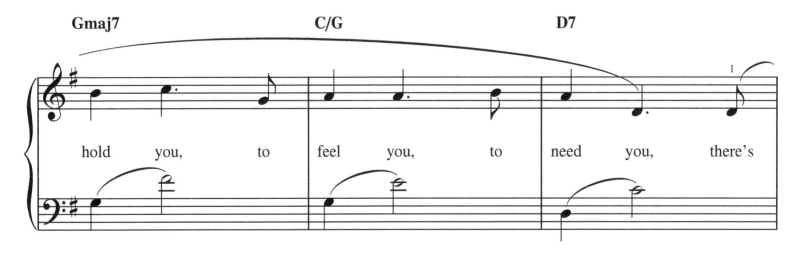

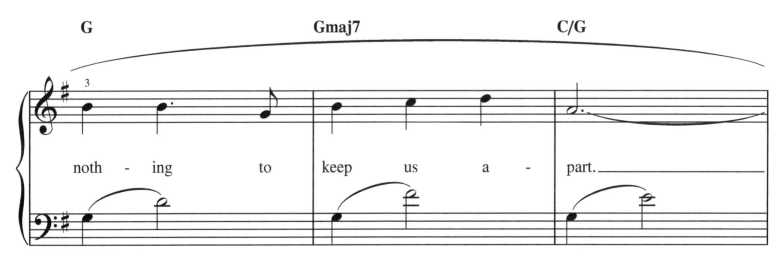

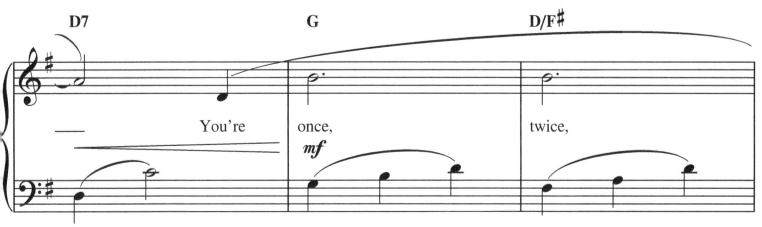

You're once,   twice,

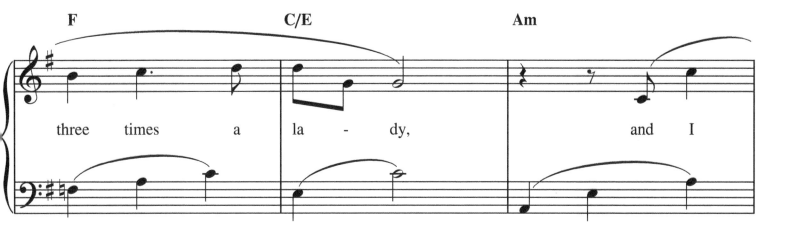

three   times   a   la - dy,   and   I

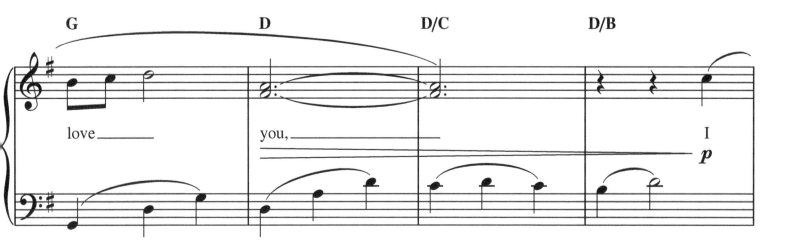

love ___   you, ___   I

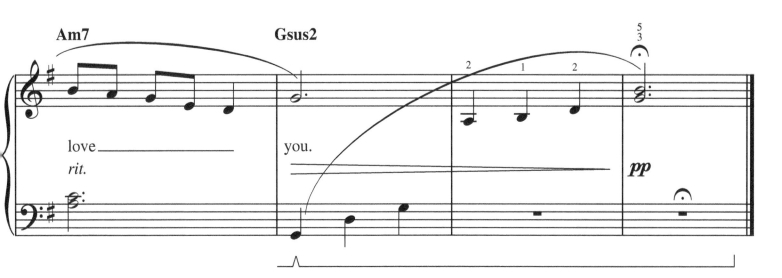

love ___   you.

YOU ARE SO BEAUTIFUL

Words and Music by BILLY PRESTON
and BRUCE FISHER
Arranged by Phillip Keveren

Slowly, warmly (♩=69)

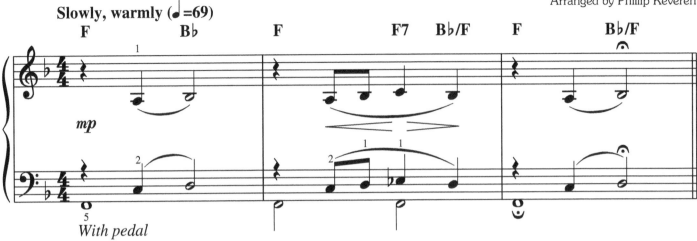

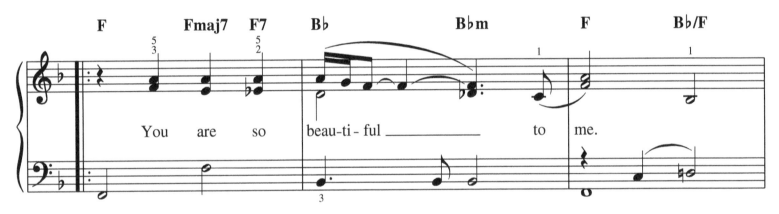

You are so beau-ti-ful _____ to me.

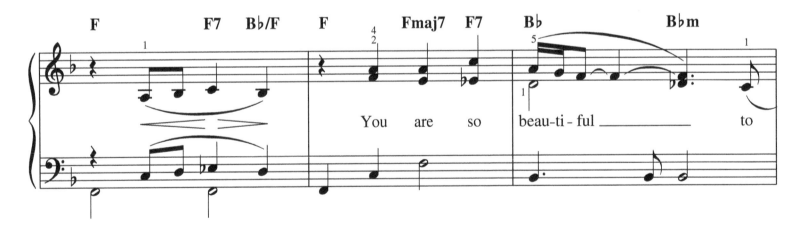

You are so beau-ti-ful _____ to

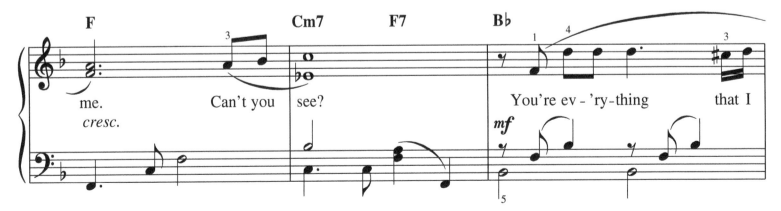

me. Can't you see? You're ev-'ry-thing that I

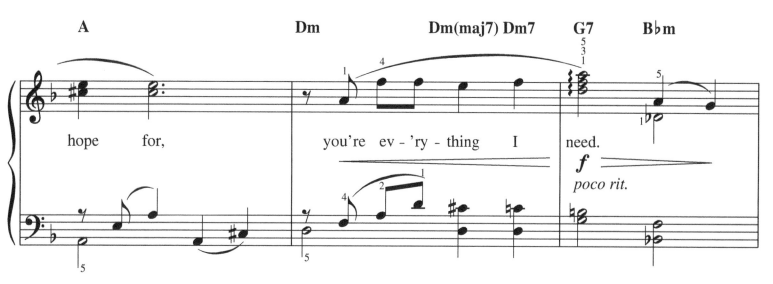

hope for, you're ev-'ry-thing I need.

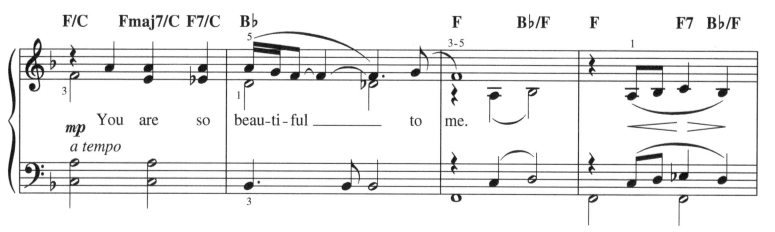

You are so beau-ti-ful _____ to me.

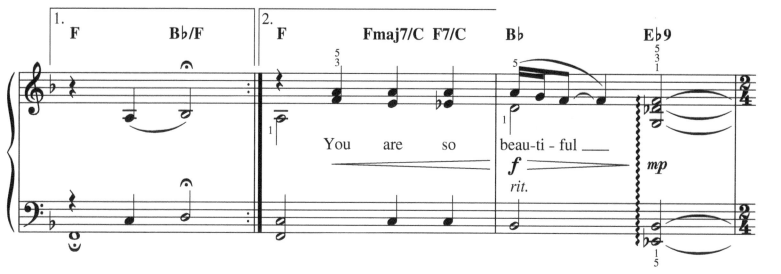

You are so beau-ti-ful ____

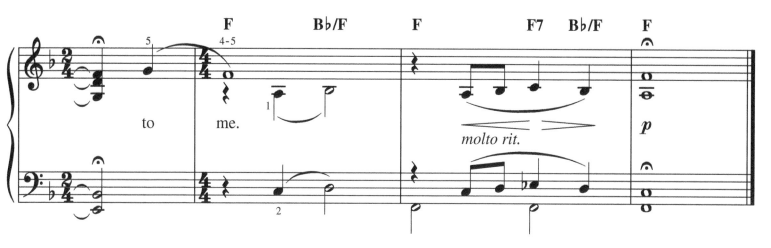

to me.

WHAT A FOOL BELIEVES

Words and Music by MICHAEL McDONALD
and KENNY LOGGINS
Arranged by Phillip Keveren

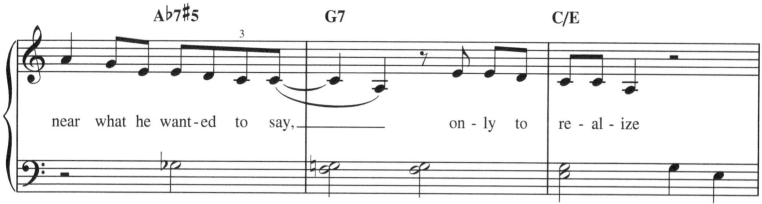

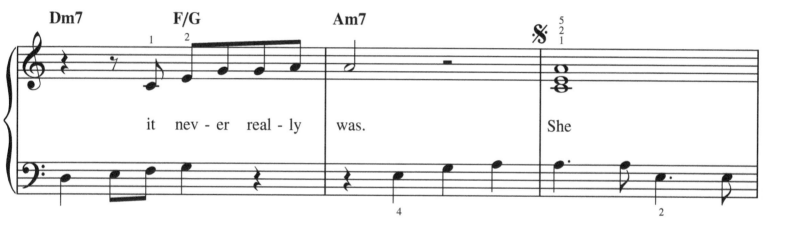

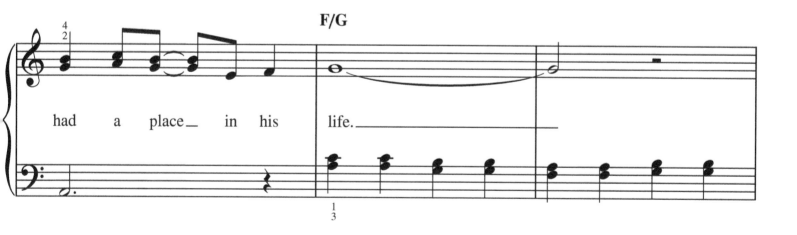

As he ris - es to___ her a - pol - o - gy, an - y - bod - y

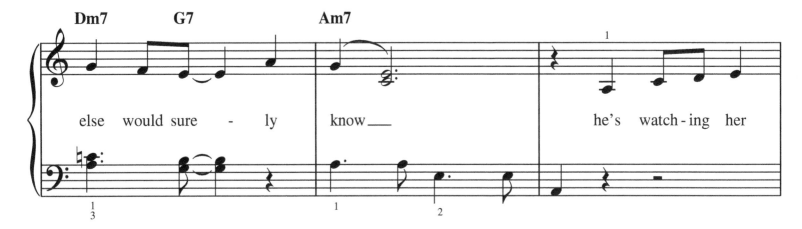

else would sure - ly know___ he's watch - ing her

go.___ But what a fool__ be - lieves___

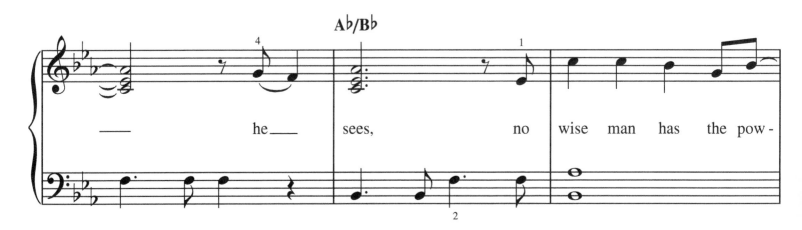

___ he__ sees, no wise man has the pow -

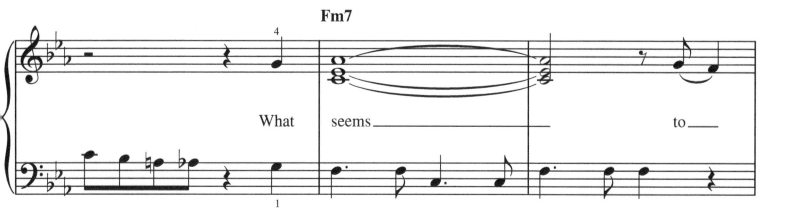

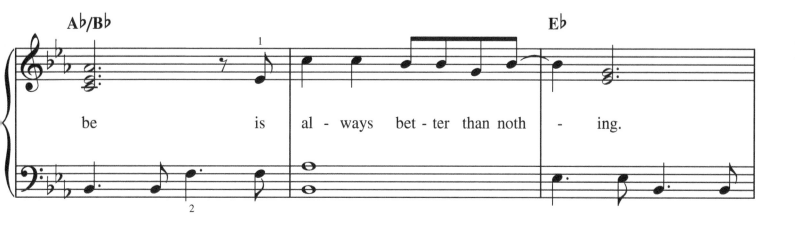

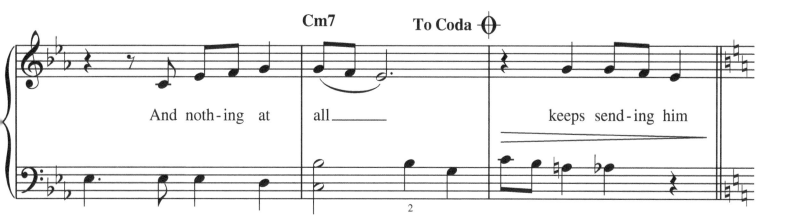

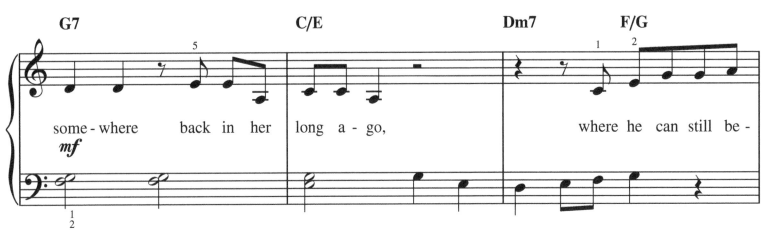

some - where   back in her   long a - go,   where he can still be -

mf

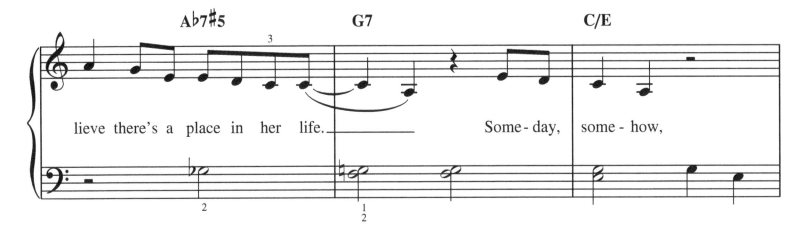

lieve there's a place in her   life.____   Some - day,   some - how,

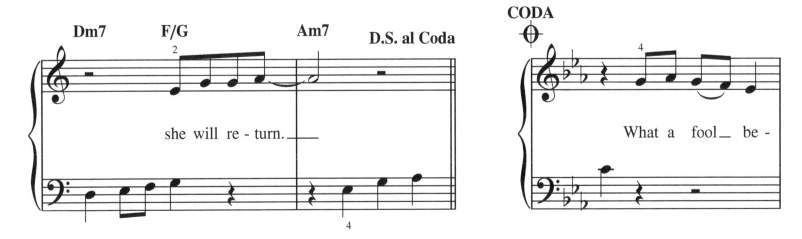

she will re - turn.____

D.S. al Coda

CODA

What a fool__ be -

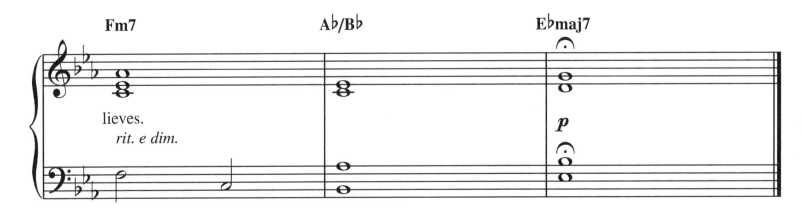

lieves.

rit. e dim.

p

THE PHILLIP KEVEREN SERIES

PIANO SOLO

ABBA FOR CLASSICAL PIANO
00156644...$14.99

ABOVE ALL
00311024...$12.99

BACH MEETS JAZZ
00198473...$14.99

THE BEATLES
00306412...$16.99

THE BEATLES FOR CLASSICAL PIANO
00312189...$14.99

THE BEATLES – RECITAL SUITES
00275876...$19.99

BEST PIANO SOLOS
00312546...$14.99

BLESSINGS
00156601...$12.99

BLUES CLASSICS
00198656...$12.99

BROADWAY'S BEST
00310669...$14.99

A CELTIC CHRISTMAS
00310629...$12.99

THE CELTIC COLLECTION
00310549...$12.95

CELTIC SONGS WITH A CLASSICAL FLAIR
00280571...$12.99

CHRISTMAS MEDLEYS
00311414...$12.99

CHRISTMAS AT THE MOVIES
00312190...$14.99

CHRISTMAS SONGS FOR CLASSICAL PIANO
00233788...$12.99

CINEMA CLASSICS
00310607...$14.99

CLASSICAL JAZZ
00311083...$12.95

COLDPLAY FOR CLASSICAL PIANO
00137779...$15.99

DISNEY RECITAL SUITES
00249097...$16.99

DISNEY SONGS FOR CLASSICAL PIANO
00311754...$16.99

DISNEY SONGS FOR RAGTIME PIANO
00241379...$16.99

THE FILM SCORE COLLECTION
00311811...$14.99

FOLKSONGS WITH A CLASSICAL FLAIR
00269408...$12.99

GOLDEN SCORES
00233789...$14.99

GOSPEL GREATS
00144351...$12.99

GREAT STANDARDS
00311157...$12.95

THE HYMN COLLECTION
00311071...$12.99

HYMN MEDLEYS
00311349...$12.99

HYMNS IN A CELTIC STYLE
00280705...$12.99

HYMNS WITH A CLASSICAL FLAIR
00269407...$12.99

HYMNS WITH A TOUCH OF JAZZ
00311249...$12.99

JINGLE JAZZ
00310762...$14.99

BILLY JOEL FOR CLASSICAL PIANO
00175310...$15.99

ELTON JOHN FOR CLASSICAL PIANO
00126449...$15.99

LET FREEDOM RING!
00310839...$12.99

ANDREW LLOYD WEBBER
00313227...$15.99

MANCINI MAGIC
00313523...$14.99

MORE DISNEY SONGS FOR CLASSICAL PIANO
00312113...$15.99

MOTOWN HITS
00311295...$12.95

PIAZZOLLA TANGOS
00306870...$15.99

QUEEN FOR CLASSICAL PIANO
00156645...$15.99

RICHARD RODGERS CLASSICS
00310755...$15.99

SHOUT TO THE LORD!
00310699...$14.99

SONGS FROM CHILDHOOD FOR EASY CLASSICAL PIANO
00233688...$12.99

THE SOUND OF MUSIC
00119403...$14.99

SYMPHONIC HYMNS FOR PIANO
00224738...$14.99

TIN PAN ALLEY
00279673...$12.99

TREASURED HYMNS FOR CLASSICAL PIANO
00312112...$14.99

THE TWELVE KEYS OF CHRISTMAS
00144926...$12.99

YULETIDE JAZZ
00311911...$17.99

EASY PIANO

AFRICAN-AMERICAN SPIRITUALS
00310610...$10.99

CATCHY SONGS FOR PIANO
00218387...$12.99

CELTIC DREAMS
00310973...$10.95

CHRISTMAS CAROLS FOR EASY CLASSICAL PIANO
00233686...$12.99

CHRISTMAS POPS
00311126...$14.99

CLASSIC POP/ROCK HITS
00311548...$12.95

A CLASSICAL CHRISTMAS
00310769...$10.95

CLASSICAL MOVIE THEMES
00310975...$12.99

CONTEMPORARY WORSHIP FAVORITES
00311805...$14.99

DISNEY SONGS FOR EASY CLASSICAL PIANO
00144352...$12.99

EARLY ROCK 'N' ROLL
00311093...$12.99

GEORGE GERSHWIN CLASSICS
00110374...$12.99

GOSPEL TREASURES
00310805...$12.99

THE VINCE GUARALDI COLLECTION
00306821...$16.99

HYMNS FOR EASY CLASSICAL PIANO
00160294...$12.99

IMMORTAL HYMNS
00310798...$12.99

JAZZ STANDARDS
00311294...$12.99

LOVE SONGS
00310744...$12.99

THE MOST BEAUTIFUL SONGS FOR EASY CLASSICAL PIANO
00233740...$12.99

POP STANDARDS FOR EASY CLASSICAL PIANO
00233739...$12.99

RAGTIME CLASSICS
00311293...$10.95

SONGS FROM CHILDHOOD FOR EASY CLASSICAL PIANO
00233688...$12.99

SONGS OF INSPIRATION
00103258...$12.99

TIMELESS PRAISE
00310712...$12.95

10,000 REASONS
00126450...$14.99

TV THEMES
00311086...$12.99

21 GREAT CLASSICS
00310717...$12.99

WEEKLY WORSHIP
00145342...$16.99

BIG-NOTE PIANO

CHILDREN'S FAVORITE MOVIE SONGS
00310838...$12.99

CHRISTMAS MUSIC
00311247...$10.95

CLASSICAL FAVORITES
00277368...$12.99

CONTEMPORARY HITS
00310907...$12.99

DISNEY FAVORITES
00277370...$14.99

JOY TO THE WORLD
00310888...$10.95

THE NUTCRACKER
00310908...$10.99

STAR WARS
00277371...$16.99

BEGINNING PIANO SOLOS

AWESOME GOD
00311202...$12.99

CHRISTIAN CHILDREN'S FAVORITES
00310837...$12.99

CHRISTMAS FAVORITES
00311246...$10.95

CHRISTMAS TIME IS HERE
00311334...$12.99

CHRISTMAS TRADITIONS
00311117...$10.99

EASY HYMNS
00311250...$12.99

EVERLASTING GOD
00102710...$10.99

JAZZY TUNES
00311403...$10.95

PIANO DUET

CLASSICAL THEME DUETS
00311350...$10.99

HYMN DUETS
00311544...$12.99

PRAISE & WORSHIP DUETS
00311203...$12.99

STAR WARS
00119405...$14.99

WORSHIP SONGS FOR TWO
00253545...$12.99

HAL•LEONARD®

Visit **www.halleonard.com**
for a complete series listing.

Prices, contents, and availability subject to change without notice.

0419
158